Dumbing Down Deer Hunting

BY

James A. Lahde Ph.D.

The Rise

and

Fall of Deer Hunting

in

Michigan

WOODCOCK PRESS
ROCK, MICHIGAN

A Woodcock Press Publication

Printed in the United States of America
ISBN 0-9658554-0-6

ACKNOWLEDGMENTS

First, I would like to thank my wife Virginia, brother-in law, Alvin Ranger and great friends Bill White, Don Moody, Jack Mellinger, Dean Alto, Waino Bakka, Ted Bartczak and John Skellinger for their comments on a early draft and their initial encouragement to pursue the bait-blind hunting theme.

A special note of thanks goes out to Pete Petoskey and John Ozoga for their knowledge and comments related to facts on wildlife management and Michigan's Department of Natural Resources

And a sincere, heartfelt thanks to Nancy Mathews for her editing skills.

The line drawings throughout the book were done by wonderful friend Mary Douse, from Birmingham Michigan.

Jim Lahde
is native to
Michigan's Upper Peninsula
with a
Ph.D in Educational Curriculum
Development from the
University of Michigan.
As a retired educator, he raises whitetail,
writes, plays a little golf, hunts and traps
as much as possible.
Other publications include:

Forest Wildlife and Ecology, Woodcock
Press: A secondary course of study in
wildlife management.

Planning For Change, Columbia University Press: A secondary course of study
in Environmental Land Planning.

*A Gourmet's Guide to Venison Sausage and Cooking
Venison*, Woodcock Press:
A guide book for anyone who enjoys using
venison to produce quality home-made sausage and
exciting gourmet dishes.

TO
THE
MAGNIFICENT
WHITETAIL

MAY
THEY FOREVER
EXCITE
INVIGORATE
PROVOKE
AND
INFLAME

TABLE OF CONTENTS

A THANKSGIVING HUNT

I'd like to see some boys
Leave home Thanksgiving Day
And once again take
Separate paths through cedar coppice
Driving dam and stag
Past others, alert
And quick to kill.
Taking the whole day
With no guilt since
Birds taste just as good on Sunday
As they did back then.
And, Mother, long gone,
Would understand,
She always did.
And Dad, beside her,
Would surely wink approval
And wish to come.

JL

Dumbing Down Deer Hunting

INTRODUCTION

What happened to hunting on Thanksgiving? Hunting the whole day with no guilt? Has it gone the way of still hunts to be replaced with mind-numbing, hypnotic staring through glassed windows at piles of bait? Has it gone the way of the vigorous drive replaced by trips on an ATV to bait the blind? Today, it seems, the male presence is needed not only to carve turkey but demonstrate the appropriate, fashionable, politically correct behavior of the caring husband and father.

A trivial matter? Perhaps, but one of the many symbolic gestures in a long litany of humanizing activities designed to civilize men. While there may be some justification in taming men's brutish nature, there are a few minor obsessions I'd like to keep and hold sacred: One is "The Hunt." And, if that means stuffing the bird on Sunday or the day after deer season then that's when the bird should be stuffed.

My real frustration is not with deer hunting on Thanksgiving but with the humiliating practice of hunting from blinds over piles of artificial bait. Not only is bait-blind hunting a blemish on the hunting establishment it represents a *huge* step in civilizing a field sport with an ageless tradition of rugged individualism.

The word "civilized" always leaves me somewhat apprehensive; it has such a benevolent tone with so many emotional overtones. In a feverish attempt to find an alternative, I searched my English (US) Thesaurus and was surprise to find the words "domesticated", "indoctrinated" and "brain-washed" among the nine synonyms. I think some hunters have been domesticated into accepting shooting baited deer from blinds as deer hunting.

The following chapters will show how and why hunting behaviors—for well over two million years—played a fundamental role in shaping not only individual behavior but social behavior as well; and how these behaviors were passed on from generation to generation by individuals predisposed to hunt, defend family and tribal resources. I have tried to illustrate why, during the Middle Ages, classical hunting styles like the still hunt, the drive, the stand and sport shoot evolved among European aristocracy; and how, during this long period of written history, universal warfare played a major role in keeping hunting behavior dominant in sedentary and hunter-gathering gene pools.

The chapter "Hunting in Colonial America" takes a brief look at the public's unfettered and unrestrained participation in subsistence hunting, market hunting, sport hunting and sport shoots during this period, practices that prevailed until the 20th century when game laws began to take effect. Then, there's a fleeting glance at deer management from the 1880s through the 1960s as rifle deer hunting in the United States took on a uniquely American form: the general public's participation in and use of classical hunting techniques.

The brief chapter on "Traditional Hunting" illustrates a typical still-and-stalk hunt carried out sometimes in the 1950s or 1960s meant to characterize these classical fair-chase techniques and offers some insight into the mystical connection they contrive between man, nature and white-tailed deer. Then, with rifle deer hunters adopting bear and bow hunter's baiting technique, we see a most amazing transformation take place in the chapters "Bait-Blind Hunting" and "Problems With Bait-Blind Hunting." The chapters reveal how traditional hunting styles were replaced by bait-blind hunting and how hunters, and the Michigan Department of Natural Resources (DNR), in adopting this practice, set aside and completely ignored the most basic principles of hunting: fair chase, the rights of other hunters and white-tailed deer plus most principles of sound game management.

There's further evidence to show how the practice encourages the spread of parasites and disease within deer herds, helps reduce quality deer hunting habitat throughout Michigan and inspires a host of illegal activities. Lengthy descriptions describe how bait-blind hunting ignores hunting standards leading to responsible stewardship in young and old hunters alike while helping, substantially, to spawn a negative image of hunting with the general public

All this devastation to classical hunting was achieved in the short span of 20-30 years. How such a remarkable feat was carried out is examined in "Hunting Redefined." The chapter on "Problems With Social Science Management" illustrates why the administration of bait-blind hunting is a classical example of how management styles, based on equal rights to one and all, are so often doomed to experience excessive policy creep and become extremely laborious and costly to implement.

In the last chapter, I suggest hunters examine their ethical and moral responsibility toward wildlife stewardship and their need for hunting standards based on a new kind of ethic: standards that set limits on what we harvest to maintain the vitality and viability of deer herds—while offering adequate "trophy" potential—and clear sociological standards on how we harvest these animals.

Finally, I hope the documentation here provides some ammunition to those hunters attempting to fight bait-blind hunting as a most demoralizing practice and elevate hunting back to its respectable past. Let's take back a little of our past, be proud of being hunters, be proud of our hunting heritage and move on to a new era of game management in Michigan. To paraphrase Denys Finch-Hatton:

If you can smell a fine cigar and not wish to inhale deeply;
If you can hear a beautiful piece of music without wanting
    to learn it by heart;
If you can see a beautiful woman without wishing to love her;
If you can see a fine specimen of game without wishing to
    take it,
You have no human heart or are hopelessly domesticated.

Dumbing Down Deer Hunting

Dumbing Down Deer Hunting

HUNTING AND WAR 🦌

E ven prior to Stone-Age man, hunting had a long history of genetic ties to lower predatory forms of life. The predator-prey relationship is one of nature's signature activities. Hunting as a universal fact transcends all levels of the biological hierarchy, from bottom to top, and all human cultures, east to west and north to south, with few or no exceptions. Where such behavior began is obscured by time but it's safe to say the genetic mechanism to hunt and kill is imbedded in all in one form or another and in some to a very high degree.

Humans are extremely malleable creatures, even more so than deer. Their pliant nature stems partly from a wonderful genetic capacity for individual diversification and partly from social interaction between individuals and groups—a dual tract of inheritance: biological and cultural. Everyone is born with physical, psychological and emotional potentials that family and culture later shape; and all have an insatiable desire to satisfy personal needs, whether real or perceived. Satisfying an insatiable diet in a world of limited resources can be difficult. To help, some species like ants, canines, lions and humans discovered the struggle is best accomplished by working together in structured, organized environments.

For more than two million years hunting was the driving force behind social evolution. In studies of hunting-gathering societies, anthropologists found that one-third the average diet consisted of fresh meat but, because meat contains the most desired fats and proteins, hunters received a special place of honor and prestige in the group.

The most current archeological theory suggests the cherished protein was shared with the extended family, thereby stimulating dialogue from which a language unique to each culture was developed and refined. In turn, the interaction between hunter and kin resulted in better technology such as the production of simple stone flakes used for skinning and carving game.

These food-sharing socials in the camps were intense, involving elaborate rituals governed by myth. In the context of social evolution, myths are defined as firmly held beliefs that help guide social behavior. So defined, religion and political beliefs, hunting ethics and social mores guiding individual and group behavior are considered myths.

The process of hunting driving language, language driving technology and technology looping back to activate hunting is unique to the human species. Except during the Dark Ages this process would be repeated over and over and over again.* During most of early human history, major biological changes also occurred, with the body achieving a more upright posture to facilitate walking; a faster, more flexible athletic body to help in hunting; and a much larger brain—three times the size of our pre-human ancestors—to facilitate language and learning skills.

About 200,000 years ago, the pace of cultural evolution picked up speed. Social interaction became more sophisticated, bands interacted with other bands forming

---

*Great examples of this progressive language-technology-loop phenomenon are TVs and microcomputers. Just think of how rapidly they changed social behavior and their effect on related technologies in the last 50 years

21

social and political networks (dialectical tribes) linked by custom and language. Labor was increasingly divided according to predisposed genetic traits. Since children require years of tutelage and near constant care, women advanced strong nurturing and bonding behaviors conducive to maintaining family continuity and cohesiveness. Others, because of their physical, psychological or emotional makeup, drifted toward harvesting wild foods, healing the sick, making tools and interpreting the unknown—each a definable, occupational niche. Over time, these adaptive behaviors were selected and strengthened as they proved beneficial to the individual or social unit.

Hunting was part of the division-of-labor scheme as well. Even in Neolithic times some 45,000 years ago, not all humans hunted. Under stress, all had the capacity to pursue and kill, but some were physically and mentally more capable than others. Anthropological evidence suggests that women and children took active roles in capturing game by setting snares and spring traps or participating in net drives, cliff drives and surrounds. Hunting as part of the food-gathering process was performed in the most efficient manner, often resembling the tactics of other social predators. Through cunning, coordination and cooperation, matching skills of wolves and other pack-hunting animals, man not only divided labor more efficiently but killed game much larger than himself, butchered and stored surplus prey, fed solid food to his young and used aggressive hunting tactics against competitors.

Since killing was carried out with club or spear, individuals born aggressive, strong, courageous, agile and clever were destined to hunt big game or participate in inter-clan or tribal conflicts. These behaviors proved successful leadership qualities as well. Over time, good leaders learned to balance hunting behavior with more compassionate, social skills that made them attractive and interesting to women, good with children, controlled and cooperative with related clans as well as eloquent, knowledgeable and skillful at tribal affairs. Evolving behaviors like anger, hate and revenge—non-endearing traits in today's society—were all extremely necessary for survival.

Valued hunting characteristics also translated into valued leadership attributes in time of war where aggression, organization, planning, protection, revenge and retribution were important goals. From the beginning, hunting and war ran parallel tracks in history: one driven by the need for a healthy diet and the other by the need for protection and, both, carried out by the same individuals.

Early man, like all animals, was either predator or prey. He killed to eat, defend territory, assert dominance or protect family, friends and treasured resources.

While social evolution was on the fast track, biological evolution came to a near standstill. Changes that did occur in the past 50,000-60,000 years were probably in brain neurology since scientists can show no outward modifications to the human body. Just as people in 1950 were like us biologically but lived in a world without TVs and computers, so the villagers of 12,000 years ago were just like us but lacked our technology and elaborate cultural infrastructure. With social and technological advancement leading the way, *Homo sapiens* slowly migrated from Africa through Europe, Asia, the Americas and Australia as successful hunting and gathering cultures.

Life for some hunters-gathers, living in the Mediterranean area, changed radically about 10,000 years ago when refinements in agriculture and animal husbandry permitted a sedentary lifestyle and the rise of cities and city-states. Here ideologies or myths become codified as religions, laws, the sciences and politics; and, universal social skills became institutionalized into recognized occupations, such as architecture, farming, the military, engineering, medicine and hunting. During this period man cultivates the soil, breeds animals, communicates by writing, wages war on neighboring states and "goes hunting on the weekend."

Some of the earliest writings on hunting show Egyptians, Greeks and Romans enjoying a variety of hunting styles. Whether using the battue—an early driving technique—to stir the red stags from cover or hounds to run down lions or prairie falcons to stun and carry grouse to ground, hunting was carried out by aristocrats with rigid standards of conduct for the chase. The Norman conquest of the British Isles brought a formalized system of laws and a highly orthodox approach to deer hunting. William of Normandy (1100 AD) is generally credited with the founding of modern hunting as practiced in England and later in the United States. Laws enacted by him and his successors on the English throne—elaborate and harshly punitive in their original framework—form the basis of our modern system of English game laws. Large tracks of forest were proclaimed reserves where hunting was permitted only with royal authority. Restricting hunting rights only to the upper class limited the practice of hunting skills for the middle class and poor to game keeper, game stalker, soldier or, for the brave, poacher.

During this period, the battue was perfected to the point where sportsmen shot driven game from stands scattered about the reserve, turning the traditional drive into a "shoot." The practice was considered more refined since it was below the dignity of the sporting elite to beat or stalk the brush for game. Game keepers became the first wildlife managers who functioned as shoot organizer or, if need be, as game stalkers and beaters. During this period, the poor and middle class raised poaching to a fine art with the perfection of traps, nets, snares and other illegal devices.

It's important to emphasis here that, although hunting as a essential food-gathering occupation was eliminated in agricultural societies, its rudimentary behaviors were expressed through aristocrats who enjoyed hunting as sport, commoners who poached for subsistence or occupation and dominant leaders, soldiers and mercenaries who used hunting skills in battle and war games. At this time in Europe, most men were under subscription to local lords, knights or kings which was not a bad deal since booty and plunder were some of the few ways peasants could achieve fortune and fame. Like prehistoric times, the world was divided into friend and foe and response to real or perceived danger was quick and emotional. Those with the most elaborate war machines were successful. Others risked annihilation. Many peaceful people were driven into extinction or assimilated into cultures of the conquerors.

The written history most American schools teach usually starts with Rome then quickly moves on to America, its discovery, settling the wilderness, the growth of our republic and our democratic system of government. We are left to believe the road from Rome to Washington D.C. was relatively smooth with the exception of the Dark Ages when everything shut down for a thousand years or more and battles were fought only to mark the passage of time. This period was, in fact, quite turbulent as "barbarians" swept down, time and time again, from the steppes of Eurasia to plunder and pillage western Europe, the Middle East, India and China.

Since early western history focused on Mediterranean cultures and their civilizing effects, we know little of the barbarian steppe people. But it's worth spending a few paragraphs on these nomads because they epitomize the degree to which hunting tactics had on world history; the supremacy of their behaviors in achieving tribal or state dominance and the relatively short period of time these behaviors have not dominated social interaction.

What little we do know of these nomads comes from history written by men of sedentary, primarily agricultural-based cultures like Rome, Persia, India and China and contains little of their nomadic life and only such events as affected the writer, which was most often murderous and brutal. Even Marco Polo's detailed description of his travels through the Mongol Empire (1271-1295 AD) and life in Kublai Khan's courts is more an account of a lifestyle much influenced by the culture conquered and not a true reflection of the steppe lifestyle. In his encyclopedic book, *THE EMPIRE OF THE STEPPES: A History of Central Asia,* René Grousset, offers brief sketches of their lifestyle but always in the context of war or battle. From the book, though, one is able to establish that the nomad was trained from childhood to ride horses; patiently stalk game; drive, rope or shoot game at full gallop, and to master all the hunter's skills. Grousset's description of the young Jenghiz Khan—Kublai Khan's father—illustrates this point well:

> The phalanx and the legion (battle formations) passed away because they had been born of the political constitutions of Macedonia and Rome; They were the planned creation of organized states which, like all states, arose, lived, and disappeared. The mounted archer of the steppe reigned over Eurasia for thirteen centuries because he was the spontaneous creation of the soil itself: the off-

spring of hunger and want, the nomads' only means of survival during years of famine. When Jenghiz Khan succeeded in conquering the world, he was able to do so because, as an orphan abandoned on the plain of Kerulen, he had already succeeded, with his younger brother Jöchi the Tiger, in bring down enough game daily to escape death by starvation.

While considered uncivilized for their murderous ways, these people were well organized politically, with a rigid social structure. Whether Turkoman, Mongol or Hun, they belonged to an intelligent, thoughtful, practical people who were driven by periodic droughts from their northern grasslands to raid and plunder neighbors to south, east and west. Though backward in material culture, they were unequaled in battle. Grousset describes their wolf-pack tactics:

> Not that he often confronted his enemy; on the contrary, having launched a surprise attack upon him, he would vanish, reappear, pursue him ardently without letting himself be caught, harry him, weary him, and at last bring him down exhausted, like driven game.

They were totally uncharacteristic in their post-conquering style as in their fighting style. Being only interested in booty, not converts, their invasions repeatedly followed the same lifecycle. When a sedentary, urbanized community yielded under their onslaught, most of the indigenous population were massacred and the nomad seated himself on the defeated ruler's throne as khan of China, king of Persia or emperor of India. Soon the nomad was assimilated and habituated—civilized—into a culture that was just as quickly plundered and pillaged by new, hungry hordes that suddenly appeared on his frontier: steppe nomad, weakened by the good life, fell victim to his long-lost cousin.

For nearly 2,000 years, these steppe people were the scourge of Europe and the Far East. They epitomized the pastoral hunter-killer. With bow and arrow, on horseback, none was their equal at the hunt or war. They gave the world the chariot, the wheel, the covered wagon, the re-curved bow and an unparalleled array of equestrian paraphernalia including saddle, bridle, mouth bit and stirrup. Each item, for its time, probably had the equivalent impact of the computer on society. But, defeat as the dominant war machine came early and suddenly in the 16th century with ascendancy of a more efficient tool of the hunt and war: gun powder.

Barbarians? I think not.

Uncivilized? Perhaps.

A people with different social mores and ethics? Without doubt.

A people that cherished life, relished the chase and reveled in the kill—a people who left behind a large infusion of their nomadic, hunter-genes throughout the gene pools of Europe, China, India, and Middle East. Not all in a population were put to the sword. Nomadic leaders recognized and greatly appreciated gifted scholars, artisans and beautiful women which is evident in Jenghiz Khan's definition of supreme joy (from a Rene Grousset quote by Rashid ad-Din, in *d'Obsson*, {History of the Mongols}): ". . . to cut my enemies to pieces, drive them before me, seize their possessions, witness the tears of those dear to them, and embrace their wives and daughters!"

In the five centuries since these horse people ceased being masters of the world, their genes for the hunt have migrated to all corners of the globe. Although there have been many wars and many conquerors since, resulting in the death of millions, none were as selective in slaughter nor left behind so many offspring. Direct descendants of these remarkable people exist and flourish on the remote steppes of Russia and northern China today, still following a pastoral lifestyle, still riding and hunting from horseback.

Critics of hunting like to insinuate that hunting and its related psychology are prehistoric dinosaurs with no relevance to the present, but such opinions deny the long history of hunting and warring and the obvious fact these behaviors are more extensive and more deeply imbedded in the human spirit than we care to admit. Long before our ancestors learned to walk upright or deserved the title of *Homo sapiens* and well through 99.9 percent of human existence, individual and collective personalities were shaped by hunting and its close cousin, war—universal traits, steeped in biological and social antiquity.

Hunting and warfare left a deep and permanent yearning in the human condition that's been carefully nurtured in the various styles of battle and hunts that survive today and, especially, in those individuals genetically predisposed and socially conditioned to such activities. Any period in the long, continuous flow of history will show that men from poor, middle and upper classes alike made hunting their happiest occupation. Expressed on battlefields or football fields, in hunting preserves or deer blind, the hunt is there: a biological need and an urging that defies logic, is resistant to change and demands cultural satisfaction.

Dumbing Down Deer Hunting

HUNTING IN

COLONIAL AMERICA 🦌

I t's safe to say from these early beginnings that hunting as a food-gathering practice or part of a war-
making scheme had universal expression among cultures
of the world. But it's important to remember the biological expressions to hunt varied even within a population as
small as the family unit—stronger in some, weaker in
others.

With the rise of chiefdoms, cities and city-states, the
practices of hunting and war became more and more detached from one another. War was institutionalized, an
instrument of policy, while hunting was ritualized, an instrument of pleasure guided by a strict code of conduct. In
civilized Europe, the evolution of hunting as a subsistence
activity to a ritualized sport spanned a period of 10,000

years. In North America, the same process was compressed into a time span of 400 years.

In historic North America, as in pre-history times, subsistence hunters and soldiers paved the way for agricultural and urban pioneers. First, came Spaniards in search of treasures and conquest. They left behind horses which the Plains Indians quickly adopted and, like the Eurasian nomads, became superb horseback hunters and fighters. The Spaniards were followed by Europeans engendered with a pioneer spirit that propelled them across the Alleghenies, down the Ohio River Valley, over the Mississippi and across the Great Plains and Rocky Mountains to the Pacific. North America was a true wilderness when the first Europeans arrived. Approximately six million native Indians, speaking about 175 languages, occupied the continent. They lived a hunting-gathering existence that had prevailed for thousands of years and, as the dominant predators, helped shape the elusive and graceful qualities of deer, elk, antelope and other big game animals.

In the beginning, most exploration by Europeans originated with hunting and trapping. The mountain men and trappers of the early 19th century were the first white men to hunt the Canadian wilderness and the virgin areas west of the Mississippi. Armed with smooth-bore, black power rifles, they were intrepid explorers as well as hunters. French and then English trappers came and took on the Indian lifestyle: they harvested beaver, otter, mink, pine marten and fisher—all traded for goods made in Europe and China. They experienced hunting in a way that is shared by only a small minority of hunters today. Moving by foot or horseback rather than ATV, sleeping on the ground rather than in camper trucks, hunting in North America was carried out as a means of survival with little impact on the resource base.

The pioneer families that followed these hardy individuals had a more drastic impact on the land. The settlers brought with them their farming and city lifestyles as well as an enormous capacity to adapt technology to a new land rich in resources. Compared to similar cultural trends in Europe and Asia, the evolution from a land influenced by scattered tribes of hunter-gathers to one dominated by thousands of agricultural communities and large urban centers was rapid. Pioneers and settlers were free to use the resources as they desired. Everywhere mature forests were cut, rivers damned and the soil farmed to meet the needs of a growing nation.

The massive changes in wildlife habitats and unregulated hunting and trapping resulted in the demise of many species. The Wild-West spirit prevailed, with no distinction made between poaching, subsistence hunting, sport hunting and sport shooting. By the mid-19th century, hunting was a major source of recreation and profit. Market hunters slaughtered millions of elk, deer, bison, and birds for food, hides and feathers. Train rides whose sole purpose was shooting buffalo while passing through the prairie were a popular form of weekend recreation.

Federal agents, ranchers, and professional hunters waged massive poisoning campaigns against hawks, eagles, grizzly bears, wolves, cougars and coyotes. In the early part of this century, government hunters with the U.S. Biological Survey—precursor to the Fish and Wildlife Service—waged systematic war on wolves, coyotes and cougars. Between 1883 and 1918, approximately 80,000 wolves were killed in Montana alone. The Eastern cougar has been extinct from the Northeast since the turn of the century as a result of these early campaigns to eliminate and control their numbers.

Turkeys, fishers, the Michigan grayling, elk, pine martens, moose, passenger pigeons and other species adapted to mature stands of old-growth forests could not survive the habitat change and hunting pressure and gradually vanished from many states; or, as in the case of the passenger pigeon, became completely extinct by 1914. The American bison was reduced from an estimated population of 60 million to a mere 600 by 1896. William Hornaday in the book, *The Extermination of the American Bison*, points out that professional white hunters, Indians and settlers killed 3,698,730 bison in just one year, 1872.

Looking back on this period, one is left with the distinct impression that sport hunting with its rigid code of ethics was dead but "the ethical hunt" was kept alive by numerous 19th century hunters and their writings such as John James Audubon ("Deer Hunting" *Ornithological Biography*, 1831), George W. Sears (*Woodcraft and Camping*), Osborne Russell (*Journal of a Trapper,* 1834-1843), Frank Forester (*The Deer Stalkers*, 1843), John Dean Canton (*The Antelope and Deer of America*, 1877), Charles Hallock (*Sportsman's Gazetteer,* 1879), Oliver Hazard Perry (*Hunting Expeditions of Oliver Hazard Perry:* 1836-1855) and Ernest Thompson Seton (*The Trail of the Sandhill Stag*, 1899).

No other field sport has such a rich history of literature dedicated to the hunt. These men are among the list of many who preached the need for adapting English sporting ethics to the American scene. Audubon's essay is unique in several ways. First, he systematically describes the three principal deer hunting methods in use then: the drive, still hunting and fire-light hunting. Second, his popularity induced many deer hunters to take up the sport as recreation. These sportsmen not only kept the spirit of fair chase alive but also helped provide the framework in which hunting regulations over the next 100 years would be based.

Later, at the turn of the century, the hunter's banner was taken up by Teddy Roosevelt, a war hero, rough-and-tumble politician, our 26th president (1901-1909), avid hunter and sportsman. He was also a recognized naturalist/scientist and writer. In 1911, for example, he published *Revealing and Concealing Coloration in Birds and Mammals*, a more than 100-page-long technical scientific article written to refute an evolutionary theory on mimicry proposed by the naturalist Abbott Thayer.

Roosevelt realized that natural resources formed the basis of our nation's economy and were limited so, along with the Frenchman Gifford Pinchot, formulated regulations defined as the doctrine of *wise use* which served as conservation's working definition through much of the

20th century. As ardent hunter and naturalist, he recognized man's place in the natural order as predator but, as our first conservationist-politician, he also knew there was a thin line beyond which the hunter should not step in pursuit of game, a line which separated the sportsman from meat hunter. However, change came slowly.

Until forest fires, market hunting, poaching and sport shooting again reduced their numbers, such species as rabbits, deer and grouse thrived on the abundant tender seedlings of second growth that followed the cutting of virgin forests. Some fires burned 2-3 million acres in one continuous burn. By 1904, white-tail deer had disappeared from Ohio. By 1927 they was practically absent from New York, Indiana and the southern portions of Michigan, Wisconsin and Minnesota.

Although states had legal power to protect wildlife and wildlife habitats, such protective measure evolved slowly. This snail-pace evolution was due primarily to the public's cavalier attitude toward the land and its resources. Confronted with "unlimited resources" and armed with a Christian philosophy that espoused domination of nature, government policy reflected the frontier attitude of Manifest Destiny. This "God-given right" attitude to subdue nature was slow to accept government restrictions but game laws eventually prevailed. In 1859, Michigan passed a law limiting deer hunting to the last five months of the year. An 1881 act made it illegal to ship deer carcasses out of state and to capture deer by using pits, pitfalls and traps. In 1895, Michigan required deer hunters to purchase a hunting license.

Fires, market hunting and poaching remained problems into the 1920s where even remote areas of Michigan's Upper Peninsula had few deer for sport hunting. Over the next several decades, deer numbers again exploded as the state made a major effort to control forest fires and passed legislation to limit hunting to bucks. By 1940, deer hunting had reached its peak in northern Michigan. Since then—except for periodic fluctuations— Michigan's deer herd has remained a viable source of recreation for hunters.

The key to today's healthy deer herds is modern game management by knowledgeable deer biologists. For many years—starting in 1938—Michigan and other states conducted extensive research on wildlife needs, their diseases, population trends, restocking programs and field ecology. These studies and many others showed the land functioned as a dynamic, living system with wildlife intimately tied to their physical environment. While struggling to satisfy a variety of resource needs by the public, Michigan biologists were able to increase and maintain healthy populations of game species. As a result, rabbits, ruffed grouse, woodcock and white-tailed deer prospered for decades.

Many of the game laws and management techniques in use today have their origin in Europe as do the classical hunting styles: the still hunt, drive and stand. The shoot as practiced by Europe's elite and America's settlers never became entrenched in America's hunting culture which probably had something to do with its snobbish reputation. While poaching remains a tradition in some quarters, the old European standards of fair chase that held sway for many centuries were adopted as America's hunting standards. Hunting—"The Sport of Kings"—became the sport of all Americans. Even the poorest farm boy carried a single-shot 22 or sling-shot to school in hopes of bringing home a rabbit or squirrel.

The great hunting success we've enjoyed in the past 50-60 years was primarily due to the combination of reasonable laws, good management and responsible hunting styles. Those of us fortunate enough to have enjoyed these years must also give some credit to great writers like Archibald Rutledge and Paul Brandreth—writers for *Out-*

door Live, Field & Stream, and *Forest and Stream* —who inspired us as young hunters with their stories of great hunts and their tips on stalking the crafty whitetail.

Dumbing Down Deer Hunting

A TRADITIONAL HUNT 🦌

I t's interesting to note from this brief history of hunting in Europe and colonial America that whenever civilized hunting cultures reached a point where game became scarce, restrictive regulations came into play and classical hunting styles became the standard of choice. The longevity of such styles says something about their credibility as tested forms of recreation and harvesting game. After all, if European hunters and game keepers were comfortable with these management tools for some six to eight thousand years and game managers and hunters in the United States were satisfied for the past 100 years, they must have some intrinsic value beyond the obvious act of killing deer.

Remarkable, too, is the fact that sport hunting during these periods was able to maintain a constancy in the face of changing technology. Regardless of the weapon available, classical hunting was always carried out in a style considered for centuries as fair and sporting. This rigid code for fair chase held true well into the 20th century with such ancient tactics as the waiting stand, the drive, the chase with hounds and the still hunt most common— hunting styles practiced by millions of hunters up through the 1960s. Let's take a look at one example of classical hunting:

Only a few years ago in Michigan, a young fellow busy with school or a father busy with work and a growing family could look forward to a vacation away from his structured lifestyle. It offered a chance to immerse himself in nature and outwit crafty white-tailed deer on their terms, in their environment, playing by their rules.

Weeks of anticipating the many twists and turns fate planned into the hunt would finally end when he left camp carrying his old reliable 30-30 Winchester at his side. Stimulated by the vigorous cold and anticipating the warmth that was sure to come with an arduous walk, he set off to that bottomland where a small stream meandered through mixed evergreen and spotted alder.

Snow had fallen the night before so the game trail contrasted sharply with its border of alder, dried goldenrod and raspberry, eliminating the need for a light. During a pre-season scouting trip, he had carefully removed every twig, branch and log from the old skid-road trail that might stick a boot or brush wool pants and coat.

Stopping to examine some tracks, he opened his coat and the top two buttons of his wool shirt to prevent moisture buildup which could be a problem when he slowed to a still hunt. He guessed the tracks were from a doe, her fawn and a much larger deer, possibly a buck, that were heading back to a hemlock knoll in the swamp after feeding in the old apple orchard.

Several weeks after the season ended last year he'd scouted that knoll noting the number of beds, their size and tracks leading to and from the area. At that time he guessed a large buck had survived the season; now he hoped those blunt-toed, wide tracks belonged to him.

His first stop was extended on entering the swamp to let his presense be accepted by the wood residents who sense his too-swift entrance into their domain. It usually takes ten minutes or so but soon a red squirrel, downy woodpecker and a bevy of chick-a-dees feel comfortable enough to continue their normal chattering, tattoing and chipping.

The respite also served to let his senses adjust to their cooler, darker, shadowy home. His search for deer sign shifted to testing the wind, looking for unfamiliar forms in the landscape like the slight flicker of an ear and safe, silent footfalls before his next few steps. Subconsciously attuned to the gentle pitch of swamp silence, he listened intently for a snapped twig or the rustle of leaves while being ever so careful to harmonize each head dip and boot placement.

Then, suddenly, the adrenaline rush as sunlight flickered off polished antlers. The sustained excitement of the stalk made it difficult for any measured control over a pounding heart and frayed nerves. Finally, the sublime exaltation immediately following the kill.

Still shaking, he rests the rifle's hammer to safe position and sits back against the nearest tree to admire the deer. Minutes earlier, they had stood eye to eye, one ready to flee, the other startled to see antler, then profile, take shape. He didn't remember pulling the hammer back nor raising the rifle but the picture of the buck in his peep sight, turning back on its tracks, is still vivid. He didn't even remember hearing the explosion for his mind shifted immediately to thoughts of a second shot, and then to thoughts of doubt: Did he miss? He only recalls flashes of white through the spruce. The heavy veil of doubt lifted when a piece of ridged bone with flesh and tallow from the shoulder blade appeared on a fallen log; a little further on the buck lay dead.

Through the years, this hunt will play over and over in his mind. Luck was on his side in picking up the sun's reflection off those antlers and all through the stalk. Without Lady Luck, the buck may have bolted with his next step or remained motionless and hidden as he drifted up wind. His focus returns to the deer. While examining the shoulders to locate the bullet's trajectory a tinge of sadness creeps in for the magnificent animal, but he doesn't dwell on it. Next time the deer will win and he will go home empty handed.

The buck extends its pleasures into camp with a traditional liver-and-onion dinner and sliced nuggets of venison tenderloin fried quickly in a mix of garlic, dry champagne, onion, apple cider and maple syrup. (The venison tenderloins—1- to 2 1/2-inches wide and 8-inches long lying alongside the backbone on the inside of a deer's cavity, just in front of the back legs—were removed, cleaned and wrapped immediately upon field dressing.)

Breaded venison chops, mashed potatoes and turnips were next on the menu followed by northern Michigan Swiss steak the next evening: all gourmet fare compared to the inevitable option of Dinty Moore stew. Then each evening after dishes, the retelling: each step embellished with a good cigar, a Strohs or coffee royale made with sharp, stringent grappa, fresh from Grandma's old still where leftover hulls, stems and seeds were distilled from grapes harvested in California and converted to wine during bird season.

This is a hunt, an intimate, almost spiritual connections between woods, whitetail and man. Here is a hunter who's been in the woods and done something; practiced a skill as ancient as the trees and rocks that border the creek; exercised persistence and showed an ability to discriminate between fair play and just plain shooting; a man who hunted and inspired, enlivened and galvanized friendships by integrating the hunt into customs of food-sharing and storytelling, rituals as old as the hunt itself.

TIME PASS US BY

Time
Pass us by
For we perpetuate the hunt
Choosing not to be disturbed.
And ...
   Change
Need not apply
For She-God Diana
Feeds our venison needs quite well.
And ...
   Progress
We don't deny
But not now
Not for spirits
Stalking woody, leafy temples.

JL

Dumbing Down Deer Hunting

BAIT-BLIND

HUNTING 🦌

M ost rifle deer hunting in Michigan today is a far stretch from the still hunt just described and the ethics it portrays. Using such traditional hunting practices as standards, sport hunters over the centuries developed a number of guidelines that, in total, define the hunting ethic. These guidelines emphasized a respect for the sport and fellow hunters; inspired and maintained a positive public image; encouraged quality game habitats and game management; insured a quality hunting experience; and emphasized fair chase.

In the past decade or so, an unprecedented increase in the use of structured blinds and artificial bait has occurred with Michigan rifle hunters. The typical blind is made from wood and resembles the old, one-hole outhouse. While some are larger and more camp-like, others are quite flimsy with bits of styrofoam and sheets of plastic held together with bailing twine. Because state law requires blinds be removed from public lands after deer season, many hunters build or purchase collapsible, fabric blinds. Some serious blind hunters build sturdy collapsible wood blinds.

Baiting is different from supplemental feeding. Supplemental feeding is a management practice in which artificial feed must be put out for a long enough period of time and in enough quality to sustain deer during the winter. The theory is that supplemental feed can result in more deer and healthier deer, a practice hunting preserves have successfully done for centuries.

Baiting is the use of artificial bait to attract deer, with sugar beets, pumpkins, apples, carrots, potatoes and corn being the most popular. Others include second-cut alfalfa and clover hay, barley, oats and commercial pelletized products specifically developed for deer. The following scenario might describe a typical 1990s Michigan deer hunt:

A day before the season opens a hunter leaves the city in his truck, stopping to pick up gas for the ATV, a 20-pound propane tank for the blind, some apples, sugar beets and corn. Then it's on to camp, hopefully in time to sight in the new 30-06 with variable nine-power scope and bait the blind. At five the next morning, he layers a new, one piece, blaze orange suit over quilted underwear and thin, sheer tights—the kind that breath. A pair of La-Crosse IceMan boots enclose wool socks covering a pair of thin nylon socks—also, the kind that breath.

The five-speed Suzuki Quadrunner with four-wheel drive and three-speed subtransmission is warming as breakfast ends. Given the machine's noise and bright lights, the quarter-mile trip to the blind is uneventful. A quick trip around the bait pile indicates only a small portion of the two bushels of apples, three pounds of corn, 20 pounds of sugar beets and five pounds of oats are missing. The oats and apples have taken the biggest hit, a detail to remember. He hopes the Doe-In-Heat scent, carefully applied to boot bottoms, will suppress any camp odors his boots leave behind. Plus, you never know, the scent might bring that big fellow in just a little closer.

The first requirement on entering the three-by-six foot blind is to light the propane heater. Next the shooting window is opened because the blind is well insulated and it won't be long before the blaze orange suit comes off. Finally, after checking to see that coffee cup, Snickers bar and headset—Rush Limbough is a welcome break later in the day—are in place, he sits back on the over-stuffed chair and lights a $7.95 Peterson Robusto. It's getting close to shooting time so care is taken to keep the glow from his cigar below the open window—a hard-learned lesson from years past. As tree, shrub and bait pile begin to take shape, a deer steps out into the clearing, some 30 paces away. No rack is evident. Probably just another doe but a careful check with the 30-06, with variable nine-power scope will ....

"The Hunt"—once considered a wonderful, necessary distractions from a busy, structured lifestyle—has become instead an extension of the same. This scenario is typical of rifle "deer hunting" in Michigan today, although variations on the theme might include a young relative or friend in the blind, size and composition of the blind, or the type of ATV, heater, candy bar and cigar.

Thirty years ago, the practice of shooting deer from a camp window was considered illegal or, at best, unethical. Knowledge that one sat in a warm shack 30-40 yards from a pile of bait would have reaped endless scorn and ridicule from hunting companions.

This is not "hunting;" it's target shooting. Where's the fair chase? Where's the thrill and intensity of the stalk? Where's the challenge of outwitting clever whitetails on their terms, in their environment, playing by their rules? The only challenge is getting a bigger bait pile and what to do with the inevitable doe, spike- or fork-horn. The whole hunt is mechanized and encapsulating, the very essence of hunting is lost.

The hunter who scouted beds, cleared trails, still hunted, stalked, shot and shared a great stag with his hunting companions earned their respect and nods of approval even as the story was repeated for a third time. The dreams he inspired among the youth in camp also served as cherished memories of the hunt-camp they aspired acceptance to. But will old-timers nod approval and understanding or youngsters stare in respect for the spike shot over bait from the window?

Bait-blind hunting crosses the line from hunting to a "shoot." President Jimmy Carter in an extremely insightful essay (*A Childhood Outdoors*, "An Outdoor Journal", 1988) makes this point very clearly:

> It is the strict circumscription of hunting and fishing—those unwritten rules of ethics, etiquette, and propriety—that define the challenge . . . not too much disadvantage for the prey . . . so that both skill and good fortune will be necessary in achieving your goal . . . Success when it comes, must be difficult and uncertain. The effortless taking of game is not hunting—it is slaughter.

In 1942, José Ortega Y Gasset, one of Spain's most outstanding philosophers, wrote *Mediations on Hunting,* a prologue to a friend's book, *Veinte Anos De Caza Mayor* (Twenty Years a Big Game Hunter). The prologue itself was published separately in 1947 and subsequently translated into German, Dutch, Japanese and eventually English. Although Ortega died in 1955, he is still considered hunting's most articulate spokesman by many leading outdoor writers in the United States. In his book he also states what hunting is not:

> To exterminate or to destroy animals by an invincible and automatic procedure is not hunting . . . (*In a foot note, he continues*) Let me be absolutely clear: I do not mean that doing this would not be hunting for sport. No, no; the fact is that it would not be hunting at all.

A shoot is any sport in which game is lured to or driven past hunters in stands or blinds. The practice is traditional in Europe's large managed reserves where game is raised specifically for that purpose. The shoot was redefined as hunting when wildlife shooting preserves became popular in this country. To define shooting deer from a baited blind or shooting driven ducks or driven pheasants as hunting can only be attributed to a bad case of guilt or a smart public relations manager.

Dumbing Down Deer Hunting

PROBLEMS WITH

BAIT-BLIND HUNTING🦌

Not only is the essence of the hunt lost but bait-blind hunting violates most tenets of a sportsman's creed. Following is an analysis of guidelines or ethical principles taken from several creeds designed to measure deer-hunting conduct. Guidelines associated with gun safety, game law and other matters not related to hunting style are not included. The guidelines were taken from various conservation organizations or hunt clubs, such as the National Rifle Association which defines a white-tailed deer hunter as one with a close tie to traditions and one for whom woodsmanship and appreciation of nature provides food for body and soul. Bait-blind hunting could not stand the hunting test judged on this one definition alone.

PRINCIPLE # 1: DEER HUNTING SHOULD PROMOTE THE PRIN-
CIPLES OF CHANCE AND FAIR CHASE

Who said "You can't build a better mouse trap?" If hunting is simply a sport of capturing game at any cost, then bait-blind hunting is the better mouse trap. Fair chase? There is no chase in bait-blind hunting and there is nothing fair about the practice. The better mouse trap metaphor is accurate only if the elements of fair chase and chance are left out of the equation. The element of chance means, first of all, that deer are able to avoid being shot— they're capable of using their numerous survival faculties to avoid danger. The most fundamental, ethical tenet of hunting is fair chase: a condition where predator and prey function freely on an even playing field, in a climate where each can see, hear, creep, crawl and hide.

Deer have virtually no means of physical defense against predators but rely upon a highly developed mechanism of sensory awareness as protection from im-minent danger. Scenting is most acute followed by hear-ing and eyesight.

Deer are totally different animals when stalked. They are not the indifferent creature one sees at a bait pile. In the bush, they are intensely alert and their response to any potential danger is an ingenious ability to melt into dense understory or disappear in a burst of speed through thick cover. Bait-blind hunting robs these majestic animals of their ability to hear, see, scent and avoid the enemy. The combination of structured blinds and piles of bait is a classic case of synergism, where the sum is much greater than the parts. The practice robs deer of all their survival skills.

In areas and years when deer are abundant, the prospect of seeing and harvesting a deer from a blind over bait is axiomatic. If deer are in the area, they will come to bait at some point in time,. The only other ingredients needed are patience and a weapon accurate to 30 paces. Little or no skill is required for the kill: simply stick the gun out the window and shoot. Even in years when deer numbers are down, baiting provides an excellent barometer of success. If the same doe and fawn show up day after day and nothing else, go home! Try someplace else! This happened to many deer hunters in Michigan's Upper Peninsula in 1997 when a combination of two bad winters, a high population of predators and an out-of-control distribution of doe permits, crop damage permits and block permits led to a severe drop in northern Michigan's deer herd.

PRINCIPLE # 2: DEER HUNTERS SHOULD TREAT DEER, ALIVE OR DEAD, WITH PROFOUND RESPECT

For centuries the definition of a good game species has been one fitted with excellent survival skills to put the hunter at a disadvantage. White-tailed deer fit this description only if chance and fair chase are involved. The concept of chance and fair chase alludes to the treatment of whitetails as objects of respect, deserving of fair chase on an equal playing field.

But there is more to that concept than fair chase. With no effort expended to find deer, no investment of time to learn their habits or to become familiar with their habitat, whitetails shot by hunters from a blind over bait are simply targets. As targets, whitetails lose not only their survival faculties but their dignity as well.

Surely, the millions and millions of dollars spent by sportsmen on game management in this state are spent not just to shoot a grouse, to shoot a duck or shoot a deer. Appreciation of game goes far beyond these animals being viewed as targets. Since cave-painting days, man valued and admired wildlife for their beauty, their strength, courage and mystical connections to other worlds, other times.

Some of the first examples of man's need for artistic expression were made by hunters, including early small ivory figures of mammoths and horses recovered from a site in Vogelherd, Germany, created by hunter-gathers approximately 33,000 years ago. About 20,000 years ago, bas-relief carvings of horses, bison, reindeer and goats were cut into rock at the Roc de Sers site in the Charente region of France. Over the next 10,000 years, Ice Age hunters perfected their art and left behind wonderfully realistic and abstract painting of animals and humans—including hundreds of portrait-like impressions of human heads (La Marche, France)—throughout the caves in Spain, France and other western European countries.

Venison—the object of the hunt for many—is not treated much better, for much is wasted. While waste in the handling of venison cannot be attributed directly to bait-blind hunting, it does reflect a general decline in hunting standards. In years past, most hunters processed their own deer or shared the task with hunting partners. Skinning and butchering were considered extensions of the hunt—similar to leaving for deer camp a week ahead of time to "get things ready."

Hides had value and the few extra bucks came in handy. Hearts were stuffed and baked. Kidneys were creamed and ladled over firm polenta. Deer liver seldom made it home but was sliced thin at camp, quick fried in bacon grease and smothered in caramelized onions. Meaty bones were roasted then simmered with vegetables to produce a rich broth—with as much or more flavor than chicken or beef broth—for gravies, marinades, soups, head cheese or jelly loafs.

A neck and shanks were sprinkled with chopped onions, carrots, several chopped celery stalks, one or two bay leafs, a dozen peppercorns, a half-dozen juniper berries, some salt and a pint of wine; then the pot set to braise for three hours on low heat during the afternoon hunt. Ribs received a similar treatment after trimming removed as much tallow as possible. My Dad, Toivo, would savor baked tallow, smearing it on fresh bread as a snack following his afternoon shift at the mine. He claimed the habit was a throw-back to Depression days and beyond, to a young life on a hard-scrabble UP farm. Today, few hearts and livers ever make it to camp. Most are left in the gut pile to feed Canada jays, weasels, foxes, coyotes, bobcats, crows and ravens. Many hides, necks and ribs suffer an unsure fate at the processing plant, as do shanks. Considered too tough for deer burger, shanks are often cast aside.

Bummer!

Shanks cooked like veal shanks taste like veal shanks.

Well ...... almost like veal shanks.

PRINCIPLE # 3: HUNTING SHOULD BROADEN PUBLIC UNDER-STANDING OF ALL HUNTING AND REFLECT ON THE POSITIVE, COLLECTIVE IMAGE OF ALL HUNTERS

Using bait-blind hunting to strengthen and broaden public understanding of hunting can only feed the anti-hunting critics. Older fellows may recall the CBS documentary, *Guns of Autumn,* that blitzed the TV airwaves in 1975. Totally biased and dripping with blood, the film showed the "horrors" of bear hunting with dogs (in of all places, Michigan's Upper Peninsula), shooting bears at dumps and gunning for exotics in hunting preserves. One can only imagine what a clever anti-hunter would do with a documentary on Michigan deer hunting from plush blinds over well-stocked bait piles. I can see it now, some 20 years after *The Guns of Autumn*, CBS brings out its latest, "unbiased" documentary on hunting, titled:

Michigan's Killing Fields

69

Michigan's Killing Fields
AN IN-DEPTH DOCUMENTARY OF BAITING AND BLIND HUNTING FOR WHITE-TAILED DEER

Scene #1: Comfortable blind
     Young couple
     Bottle of wine
     7mm Remington with variable scope.

Between snuggles and guzzles the two take turns killing a young, beautiful doe and her fawn. After close-ups of gutting the poor, innocent animals amid a pile of pumpkins—one with a Halloween face—the camera crew packs up and drives a quarter mile to another blind where six bushels of apples lure in more innocent deer and......(you fill in the details)....... Then the camera crew packs up and drives another quarter mile to a nice new cedar-log blind, 50 yards from two tons of potatoes and sugar beets and......(you fill in the details).......

How quickly we forget!

Although the above scenario on bait-blind hunting is a bit exaggerated, little embellishment is needed to create an image the public would find deplorable and register all hunters, at best, on the level of trophy hunters or Neanderthals. Richard Smith—a popular Upper Peninsula outdoor writer—in his book "Deer Hunting," offers a whole chapter on sportsmanship and hunting ethics in which he describes what is and what is not sportsmanlike conduct. "Hunters who view hunting primarily as killing . . . and feel they must get a deer at all cost, can't be ethical or sportsmanlike. These individuals miss out on the true benefits of hunting. Hunting's primary benefit is recreational: simply to be in the outdoors; to relax in space unconfined by walls and building; to see, hear, experience, and learn about the many aspects of nature. Learning about deer, respecting deer, is a major part of deer hunting; shooting a deer is of minor significance." While some might debate whether hunting's primary purpose is recreation or a necessary tool to regulate deer populations, few can argue the wisdom of respecting nature and maintaining a positive image before the public.

PRINCIPLE # 4: DEER HUNTING SHOULD PROVIDE A QUALITY OUTDOOR EXPERIENCE WITH A CHERISHED RESPECT FOR NATURE

Since bait-blind hunting is carried out inside a blind, it cannot be considered a priceless outdoor experience. There may be some appreciation for nature but no more so than looking out the kitchen window. In addition, bait-blind hunting creates a number of environmental problems none of which illustrate a respect for the sport or nature.

Practitioners use ATVs to carry building materials and bait to hunting spots, generating noise and ugly scenes while increasing universal access to remote, wilderness areas. Litter left behind from bait has little long-term effect but is unsightly as are the thousands, perhaps millions, of vacated, dilapidated old blinds that junk-up the woods. And, what can be said about shooting lanes cut out on public land?

Double bummer!

The loss of a quality outdoor experience may be best illustrated with a discussion of buck fever. Years ago, one of the most memorable elements of deer hunting experienced by all young hunters was buck fever. I cannot recall any serious hunter who did not suffer from the problem at one time or another. A few never conquered the dreaded malady. It's also been my experience that the extreme buck fever I felt as a young hunter, and the more subdued shakes that occur today, are not duplicated in a blind. Perhaps such reaction is more a function of age but I think not. Seldom is buck fever discussed today even among novice blind hunters.

One can only speculate on the reason for this loss, but I believe it has something to do with the disconnection young bait-blind hunters have with classical hunting.

Traditional hunting is more personal with an intimate relationship between man, nature and deer. Years ago a young hunter was often on his own in the woods, alone to learn woodlore and deer habits. Some, like survival skills, came with cold and wet feet, blistered ears, near-frozen fingers and a profound belief in and respect for a *good* compass. Lessons in the best times to hunt, the effect of wind, the value of silent walking, the merit of a deft approach when stalking and the benefits of last-hour endurance and patience were passed down by dad, brother or friend but set hard to memory with snorts, flashing tails and a frustrated young man determined not to make the same mistake again.

Other lessons like working a bedding area or driving for a standing buddy were a bit more sophisticated, involving a thorough knowledge of the territory and a feeling for those special places deer hide. I think the intensity, anticipation and tension these efforts generated exploded as buck fever when "the time" finally arrived. And who says the kill isn't important. I don't know of anyone who suffered from buck fever by watching deer from a window or taking its picture. Maybe the blind, the bait and four-wheeler act like umbilical cords connecting young hunters to camp—and by extension to their urban environments—where, comfortable and relaxed, deer viewed through windows are little more than TV animations.

PRINCIPLE # 5: NO HUNTING PRACTICE SHOULD SPREAD OR THREATEN TO SPREAD WILDLIFE DISEASES

Concentrating animals in small areas could be a major problem in spreading disease and parasites. For example, bovine tuberculosis (TB) among white-tailed deer is a serious problem, with the potential to become a nightmare. Infection is spread by crowding, close contact with other deer and by repeated contact. TB has gained a toe-hold in deer on large hunt-club properties—in northern Michigan's Alcona, Alpena, Montmorency, Oscoda and Presque Isle counties—where intense winter feeding occurred. It could turn into an even greater disaster if the disease spreads to dairy cows and beef cattle.

Except for the TB problem, little evidence exists to suggest baiting causes health problems for deer, but parasitic infections can increase by crowding and close contact. Deer are subject to a number of parasites, the most well known being brain worm, lung worm and liver fluke, all of which have complicated lifecycles involving several organisms. Deer become infected by ingesting infected vegetation or organisms, like grasses and snails. Concerned biologists and preserve operators feel that concentrating deer, especially in warm weather, drastically increases the potential for parasitic, health-related problems. The potential for parasitic problems is serious enough for preserve owners to de-worm their herd several times a year.

PRINCIPLE # 6: DEER HUNTING PRACTICES SHOULD NOT DISRUPT NORMAL DEER BEHAVIOR

Many people will argue baiting does not disrupt deer movement or their normal behavior but most professional wildlife biologists and managers of large hunting preserves disagree. A survey of Wisconsin wildlife managers and wardens found that 73 percent believe baiting changes deer behavior both on a short-term and long-term basis. In autumn, deer focus on storing up fat resources for winter so quality food and its availability is of prime importance. Plus, deer are opportunists, taking advantage of available food sources and quickly becoming habituated to concentrated sources and victims of their own appetites. Anyone using timers to distribute feed will vouch to deer adjusting their feeding to timed-released bait.

Dr. James C. Kroll, in his book *A Practical Guide to Producing and Harvesting White-tailed Deer* recommends the use of natural blinds over permanent blinds mainly because "bucks quickly become conditioned to permanent stands. They adjust their activity patterns and habitat selection to reduce the probability of encountering a human. My experience has shown that bucks quickly learn the location of a stand, and take avoidance maneuvers by the third day of occupation by a hunter. Stands that have been in the same location for years are avoided entirely by mature bucks." It is also common knowledge among preserve managers and deer hunters who own and hunt large tracts of land that deer populations are increased and concentrated by year-round feeding. Where this occurs, feeding stations are scattered to alleviate the problem.

Many hunters claim deer shift to night feeding during hunting season. This observation is supported by large preserve managers who claim frequent shooting and harassment throughout the day make deer very wary, especially whitetail which are the most high strung of all members of the deer family. In the fall of 1997, my brother took 82 photographs of deer at several bait stations in an area that suffered a severe drop in deer numbers. The stations in the study, which had been relatively productive in years past, showed few deer and only one buck that, when present, fed between midnight and 2:00 AM. Such limited data are far from being statistically significant, but they lend credence to the popular belief that many deer shift to night feeding during hunting season, especially older bucks.

PRINCIPLE # 7: HUNTING SHOULD NOT DESTROY DEER SOCIAL STRUCTURE

In order to provide some degree of quality deer hunting, deer specialists recommend as adequate a buck-to-doe ratio of 1:2 or 1:3 for most herds. They also claim the mythical 1:1 ratio is not realistic even in the best of circumstances. Except for some small, isolated pockets of habitat, Michigan's buck/doe ratio has never been anywhere close to a 1:3 ratio and bait-blind hunting has not helped while its effect on mature bucks has been especially dramatic.

There's a combination of factors at work here: First, harvest practices that emphasize shooting bucks and the unregulated use of bait-blind hunting. The use of bait or blind by themselves are somewhat innocuous, harmless, inoffensive, but together, in great numbers and operating for months, they conspire to effectively reduce the number of older bucks and younger bucks significantly. Bucks will always be targeted over does and big bucks over small bucks. Michigan's deer harvest policy permitting the harvest of bucks with antlers over three inches and a variety of second buck tags does not help. A buck's chance of survival is slim when bait and blinds are scattered across his home range from October to the end of December.

The few older bucks that seem to have sixth and seventh survival senses can fall to bait and blind as well, especially as the practice becomes more and more prevalent. Every hunter knows a buck—especially young bucks—on a hot doe will follow her around, over, under or through a pile of sugar beets. Under such pressure, bucks rarely have the chance to live beyond three years of age. Plus, when pressed, every hunter will admit that many beautiful animals are taken from blinds between sundown and sunrise with lights. These problems are exaggerated in northern Michigan where bucks must live to five and six years of age to carry heavy, large racks compared to areas in southern Lower Michigan where some bucks are well endowed at age three.

Michigan's buck-harvest practices do a disservice to a herd's internal social structure as well. Recent studies carried out—primarily in southern states—indicate the presence of older bucks has a significant effect on the length of breeding seasons and the health of immature bucks. Apparently, their presence and sign—rubs and scrapes—stimulates does to be receptive earlier, therefore reducing the rut by half in some cases.

Reducing the rut by 30 or 40 days has profound effects on the health of mature bucks in winter—when they are more receptive to starvation and predation—and gives fawns an important head start in summer. Their presence and sign have a reverse effect on young bucks by reducing their testosterone level to a non-competing level, thereby rendering them better able to survive winters and mature faster.

Whether or not the same herd dynamics exists in northern herds is in question. John Ozoga—a foremost authority on northern white-tails—states that "While older buck sign suppresses the behavior of younger bucks, there is no evidence that the presence of rubs and scrapes stimulate does to breed earlier in the Upper Peninsula of Michigan. My enclosure studies showed no difference in breeding dates whether sires were mature or of yearling age."

So questions remain, but when we allow, even condone, harvest regulations that inherently remove mature bucks as a functional part of deer ecology, we need to re-examine our objectives. Permitting the deer's highly evolved breeding ritual to practically disappear from many portions of Michigan is not good game management.

PRINCIPLE # 8: A HUNTING PRACTICE SHOULD NOT REDUCE QUALITY DEER HUNTING HABITAT

The high number of big bucks taken from farm country in Alberta, Canada, in southern Michigan and from big preserves are all older animals living mainly on large tracts of protected, private land. The number of these remote, safe areas in northern Michigan capable of producing big, old bucks is few and far between today.

Northern Michigan contains hundreds of square miles of state, federal and commercial forest lands that attract deer hunters from all over the United States. Because of their expanse, these lands contained numerous remote areas offering an opportunity for quality traditional hunting and limited blind hunting. In the past few decades, however, owners and management agencies opened these areas for logging and recreation, making them accessible to four-wheel-drive trucks and ATVs. In fact, hardly a section of the state, including the Upper Peninsula, could not be traversed on foot from one road to another in an hour or two by a man with a good compass.

In addition, I firmly believe that bait-blind hunting promotes the subdivision of northern recreational lands into smaller and smaller plots, and in the process, reduces the amount of good deer hunting habitat. For example Rock, Michigan, (Delta County) is typical rural UP hunting country that's partitioned into roughly 20-acre, 40-acre and 80-acre blocks. Many medium-size farms that once dotted the area, providing security for bucks, were subdivided into smaller plots over the years as were many large forested tracts held by private and commercial interests. Smaller acreage has the advantage of being economical yet functional as bait-blind hunting property; the average hunter can afford a forty or two that will harbor several deer.

Collectively, these small parcels of hunting land— each with new access roads, ATV trails, food plots, camps, outbuildings, blinds and bait piles—take on the characteristics of some large suburban subdivisions and lose their wilderness hunting characteristics. While they still contain large numbers of deer, the quality of deer and the quality of hunting is lost or extremely limited.

81

Deer, given limited protection, quickly adjust to most natural and man-made environments—including most suburban environments where they survive very well to the point of being pests. In fact, Michigan's deer herd has undergone remarkable growth in spite of habitat lost to logging, recreation and development. So, deer hunters and biologists should be concerned for the loss of *quality hunting habitat* as much as for the loss of deer habitat.

PRINCIPLE # 9: HUNTERS SHOULD RESPECT THE RIGHTS OF OTHER HUNTERS AND NOT BE DIVISIVE TO THE HUNTING COMMUNITY

In Michigan as well as Wisconsin, baiting has polarized hunters. Surveys initiated several years ago indicated hunters were equally divided in support and opposition, but once the practice of bait-blind hunting started, it quickly spread because hunters believed they must have a blind with bait to compete. Michigan DNR's surveys conducted in 1984 and 1991 showed baiting increased from 29 percent to 41 percent, respectively, and the amount of bait jumped from 3.25 million bushels to 13.12 million bushels. There's no recent data to indicate increases over the last six years. Anecdotal evidence indicates the activity has increased dramatically.

In good hunting areas of southern Marquette, Delta and Menominee counties, it is not unusual to count 15-20 bait piles and wooden blinds per square mile. Hunting on 20 or 40 acres several years ago was incomprehensible. A quick drive or a slow, still hunt would move most of the deer to the next 40 in short fashion, but baiting permits successful hunting on one acre.

Such high concentration of bait and blinds can impact hunting in several ways, even on private land. Some folks buy small plots and a small beat-up trailer as a blind, but splurge on large bait piles; some buy 40 acres plots and put blinds on all four corners. Corner blinds on private property functionally reduce a neighbor's use of his property by 10 or 20 acres, depending on vegetative density. Infringement on neighbor's property rights is not limited to private property. Blinds on public lands that border private land have the same effect.

In the past few years, hunters discovered they can protect a favorite public hunting spot by building permanent blinds on the site, effectively eliminating 10-20 acres or so from public access. These large blocks of state, federal and commercial land become the "private property" of one hunter for two weeks or a month if the person hunts with a muzzle-loader.

State and federal regulatory agencies attempted to alleviate the problem by requiring blinds be taken down at the end of each deer season. Some crafty individuals still manage to dodge the law by marking "their spot" with break-down blinds they tuck under a nearby tree and/or pre-baiting the site for weeks prior to deer season. Some block access to interior acreage by audaciously placing their blinds on or near a trail or old skid road.

Probably the most egregious violations occur as less and less land is available for other forms of hunting. Amazing as it seems, blocks of *good* hunting land a square mile or even a half-square mile without blinds are extremely difficult to find. Unless one knows the country well, the odds of finding a place to still hunt or drive are slim.

When the thousands and thousands of "temporary" bait-blinds are added to the thousands of bait-blinds on private property—not to mention bait piles behind rural homes, camps and cottages—the total square miles they occupy and influence are staggering. As mentioned, many areas of the state have one bait-blind per 20-30 acres. Under such conditions, it is nearly impossible for the still hunter to assess deer travel patterns much less still hunt or drive. It gets so bad that pre-season scouting must be taken literally and carried out one or two days before the season starts to identify the temporary blinds and instant bait piles that spring up like so many fall mushrooms.

There's even heated debate over volume of bait. It's difficult to imagine the rancor and hostility in such discussions but apparently the battles raged in Wisconsin until regulations were passed to limit bait to ten gallons per day per blind.

Ten gallons?

How's a guy suppose to hunt with only ten gallons?

A clear invasion of privacy.

Call the attorney!

Michigan, obviously more progressive and tolerant of individual rights, imposes no such restrictions. Tons can be used and such applications are common. Such controversies do nothing but add to the many contentious disputes that already exist between hunters. Hunters using dogs in the chase consistently are accused of failing to consider the rights of property owners; rifle hunters complain bow season is too long, too disruptive to deer behavior and bow hunters harvest and wound too many deer; bow hunters tell rifle hunters to "Get bent;" musket hunters complain their season is not long enough; older bow hunters gripe they need easier access to cross-bows and, to top it off, enough hunters complained that ground blinds are not good enough, so the Natural Resource Commission approved the use of elevated blinds. Such contentious debates serves no one well especially when the hunting fraternity as a whole has suffered so long from disorganization and the inability to speak in a unified voice.

PRINCIPLE #10: HUNTERS SHOULD HELP INITIATE NOVICE HUNTERS IN THE SPIRIT AND ETHICS OF FAIR-CHASE HUNTING

It should be enough to say, regarding initiating young or novice hunters into the sport of bait-blind hunting, "God forbid!" Another generation of baiters can only exacerbate the problem; woodlore would go the way of stalking and civility the way of fair chase. Producers of compasses and insulated boots would bypass Michigan as a retail or wholesale market while the sales of headsets, coffee, Snickers bars, lounge chairs and propane heaters would skyrocket.

On a more somber note, initiating young people into bait-blind hunting is a serious concern. To the extent that bait-blind hunting prevails and endures, successive generations of hunters will be less and less capable of judicious stewardship, not only with deer but with all our resources. How much feeling and knowledge toward nature or the land's carrying capacity can one extrapolate from sitting in a blind? How can an appreciation or knowledge of deer habits be acquired unless tracks are followed, scrapes and rubs studied, bedding sites identified, browsed branches checked and a thousand other details studied?

Unless one crosses creeks on wind-blown logs or tight-wire walks a beaver dam or skirts a clearing by way of blackberry brambles, how does one get acquainted with a deer's larger home, its range? How can the subconscious formulate and internalize any emotional attachments with nature when its many subtle sounds are never heard, its ever-changing kaleidoscopic of colors never seen, and its sometimes gentle, sometimes brutal breezes never felt? Will someone fed a consistent diet of bait and blind have the sagacity and acumen to challenge DNR officials on agency policy or work tirelessly for a conservation cause? It's incomprehensible that a young boy or girl can advance strong feelings of stewardship for deer and the land by running back and forth to a blind.

PRINCIPLE # 11: ETHICAL AND QUALITY GAME MANAGEMENT SHOULD BE THE GOAL OF ALL HUNTERS

Quality deer management (QDM)—a concept that has been around for some 20 years and proven successful in many states—is being discussed today by Michigan's DNR and some Michigan sportsmen. Al Brothers and Murphy E. Ray Jr. originally popularized the concept in their 1975 book, *Producing Quality Whitetail*. They believe that "quality deer management involves quality bucks, does, fawns and habitat." In the broadest terms, quality management means harvesting bucks and enough antlerless deer—in the right proportions including fawns—to sustain a healthy population for the existing habitat. The end result would be *less* deer but a fair chance for hunters to harvest quality 2.5- or 3.5-year-old bucks that best represents the potential for their age class and habitat and a better than normal chance to harvest trophy (4.5+-years old) bucks.

The major reason many hunters look to quality deer management is the gross disparity in age with bucks (not enough older bucks) and the large disparity in sex (too many does and fawns) that exist in Michigan's deer herd. Some disparity existed before the increase in bait-blind hunting—due mainly to our young-buck harvest policy—

but bait-blind hunting makes any viable solution through quality game management much more difficult unless harvest regulations are changed to bring these ratios in line.

Sad to say, most quality deer management literature has little to say about ethics hunting. The Quality Deer Management Association lists as its goals: 1) restraint in harvesting young bucks, 2) adequate harvests of adult does, 3) sportsmen assuming responsibility in properly managing deer, 4) safe and ethical hunting and 5) education of hunters and non-hunters toward a better understanding of wildlife management.

Assumptions are made throughout their literature that getting a deer population healthy, productive—including improvements in the age structure of bucks and sex ratios—and in line with its range will automatically create a quality, ethical hunting experience. The literature fails to discuss what is meant by ethical hunting or how we harvest. Discussions with QDM members indicate the use of blinds and bait are appropriate and not serious issues with their organizations.

Karl Miller and Larry Marchinton assembled the expertise of some of the most knowledgeable white-tailed biologists across North America in their 1995 book,

Quality Whitetails. In the 321 page book, 14 lines were dedicated to baiting, the essence of which states: "Proponents (of baiting) claim the practice accomplishes harvest goals more easily with fewer hunters. . . We feel that baiting rarely has a place as a management tool. Doe harvest can probably be done more effectively with food plots and other habitat improvements. In this way, the herd benefits at the same time harvest efficiency improves. Another concern is that many believe baiting is not ethical and it therefore lends ammunition to anti-hunting groups." It will be interesting to note how quality deer management associations across the country handle the question of ethics.

PRINCIPLE # 12: HUNTING PRACTICES SHOULD NOT INSPIRE UNETHICAL OR ILLEGAL ACTIVITIES

Wisconsin's Department of Natural Resources reports that some game wardens estimate 43 percent of their time prior to deer season and 73 percent of their time during the season is spent on blind/baiting-related work. Conflicts between hunters arise over ownership of blinds, safe distances between blinds, placement of bait and blinds and the direction in which blinds face. Conflicts between land managers and bait-blind hunters are usually the result of cutting trees and shrubs, littering and trespassing by hunters and their vehicles.

While some of these problems are grossly unethical and some outright illegal, they are all significant and symptomatic of the larger problem: bait-blind hunting. In the past, bait-blind hunting was never considered an accepted hunting practice. Even Safari Club International had trouble justifying the practice among its trophy-hunting members. It's always been considered a deviant hunting style.

Some problems occur in a more subtle but just as significant fashion. The most notable are changes in the moral code that exists between hunters: social influences—peer-group pressure—hunters have on one another. Certain hunting codes are deemed important enough to be written into legislation as game laws and enforced by law enforcement officers. License fees, bag limits and shooting times fall into this category. Other ethical practices, though unwritten, are just as important because they help govern conduct that, if left unchecked, is potentially destructive to the sport. Game law compliance, respect for fellow hunters and property rights, the appreciation of and desire to maintain quality deer habitat fall into this category. These unwritten mandates are primarily enforced by hunters with self-imposed codes of conduct.

To what degree individuals and camps subscribe to these written and unwritten values has an enormous impact on local deer populations. If violating becomes accepted behavior by a majority of hunters, then deer numbers will always be difficult to regulate. Social scientists tell us the degree to which individuals or groups are willing to abide by written and unwritten rules is primarily a function of public pressure and peer pressure. This is especially true with hunting, where many unwritten codes prompt conformity to the behaviors of others because their behavior is our only guide to appropriate action.

A few years ago, when shooting from buildings was considered illegal, peer pressure to observe the rule generated compliance more than fear of being fined. Sure the occasional deer was shot from the camp door or window, but the practice was usually carried out to procure camp meat or that rare buck that "happened by." Hunters then—like hunters today—will observe the law most of the time if the rules are clear and reasonable. By condoning bait-blind hunting—once considered a vice—Michigan's DNR elevated the practice of shooting deer from buildings to the level of a virtue, just like that . . . from vice to virtue.

In the process, a restrictive peer-pressure yoke was replaced with a halo.

What a break!

No more guilt.

No more fear.

Perhaps there should be a Principle #13 that states: Thou Shall Not Make Legal That Which is Illegal. Regardless, most everyone jumped on the bandwagon, leaving behind civility toward fellow hunters, respect for white-tailed deer and an open door to public castigation.

The speed at which deer hunters adopted the practice and the speed of transformation from vice to virtue is one of the most depressing yet interesting aspects of bait-blind hunting. It's depressing because so many hunters lost sight of an ethical code giving hunting credibility while elevating it to a level of dignity that is so difficult to achieve in rifle hunting today. Both pride and dignity are difficult to achieve.

It wasn't always that way. Hunting in it purist form is an individual sport, a hunter against a resourceful animal, a wonderful game, an affirmation of man's place in nature that never fails to instill a degree of self-assurance and self-respect in those who play by the rules.

The speed of adoption is interesting too because it illustrates how radical change, affecting many thousand of individuals and groups throughout a large state, can occur without fanfare and without written legislation; all of which begs the question: How could such a cancerous practice come to dominate rifle deer hunting in a state with an agency well-known for managing natural resources? The answer to that question has to do with leadership.

JHINGACHGOOK IS DEAD

In Michigan
The spirit of Jhingachgook
Lies in state
The victim of apathy
Complacency and bait.
Yes, Jhingachgook has died
And with him went the stalk and drive
But, his urban sons survive
Where on stamp-sized plots
They strive
To lure the mighty six-point buck
With rattle, grunt, bait and luck—
Yes, Jhingachgook has surely died.

JL

Dumbing Down Deer Hunting

HUNTING REDEFINED 🦌

I f bait-blind hunting does not subscribe to any of the previously listed principles of hunting, then it cannot be classified as hunting. Bait-blind hunting crosses a line in which there is absolutely no other way to describe the practice except as a shooting sport. It even stretches the imagination and definition of a shooting sport because it's like shooting ducks on a pond. Although ducks are shot on water, no serious hunter would admit to the practice. Let's face it, deer shot from blinds over bait are "sitting ducks" and anyone attempting to define the practice as hunting or a shooting sport has a serious semantics problem. Ortega addresses this question succinctly:

> . . . as the weapon became more and more effective, man imposed more and more limitations on himself as the animal's rival in order to leave it free to practice its wily defenses, in

97

order to avoid making the prey and the hunter excessively unequal, as if passing beyond a certain limit in that relationship might annihilate the essential character of the hunt, transforming it into pure killing and destruction. Hence the confrontation between man and animal has a precise boundary beyond which hunting ceases to be hunting.

If bait-blind hunting does not subscribe to traditional principles of hunting, then it must have been redefined by someone or some organization. This is exactly what happened over the past 20 to 30 years. Sad to say, the leadership on this crusade has been Michigan's DNR.

At one time many years ago, our DNR was a small, compassionate agency called the Conservation Department. It was a "woods and water" agency, primarily concerned with Michigan's fish, forests and wildlife. The law enforcement officer was simply know as "the Conservation Officer," and everyone who fished and hunted was well acquainted with him. He was constantly in the field, checking bag limits and licenses. The fellows I remember were nice guys with great personalities who might stop by the deer camp for a cup of coffee, a story and leave behind respect for the man and his job.

For many years, Information and Education personnel functioned only to promote the cause of conservation, especially with educators. They sponsored long summer workshops for teachers and shorter weekend ones through the school year; they helped in elementary, secondary and college-level classrooms and produced endless volumes of good materials for teacher and public alike.

Until the department dropped its deer research program, it was considered one of the best wildlife research departments in the country. It was a time when the department's clientele was small, its goals clear and their implementation carried out *with authority* in a relatively smooth and carefree fashion. Such an agency was easy to admire, simple to evaluate and hold accountable.

That's not the case today. Today the DNR is a huge bureaucracy. The responsibilities it took on over the years included ground water, surface water, soil and air—some of these responsibilities eventually being taken over by the Department of Environmental Quality. Plus, the wildlife division expanded its original directives to include recovery programs for predators, turkeys, moose and elk while protecting endangered plants and wetland and many other functions.

As the agency grew, its relationship with hunters became more tenuous. The bond once connecting conservation officers, fishermen and hunters into a brotherhood was severed, replaced by suspicion and animosity. Often caustic battles erupted, such as the heated debates over bounties on predators and the decades-long controversy over shooting does. While shooting does and fawns proved an efficient way of controlling population numbers, the effect of predators on game species like deer, hares and grouse is still a debatable issue.

Throughout these long years, the agency showed leadership in the face of strong opposition from both public and political arenas. They maintained a clear focus on good resource management practices while insuring quality hunts and, in the process, exemplified strong authority and good stewardship toward the resource base.

Michigan's deer harvest policy has always operated around the core principle of harvesting bucks with antlers over three inches and the use of various limited forms of antlerless permits. Since yearlings and 2.5-year-old animals form the bulk of a normal population, harvesting bucks in this age class has the advantage of providing the largest number of hunters with venison.

About 25 years ago, some biologists were beginning to compare Michigan's deer management policy to the relatively new quality-deer-management theories that espoused quality bucks, does and fawn in balance with their environment and in harmony with their social structure. On appraisal, they questioned a policy permitting disparate ratios of does to buck, young bucks to old bucks and excessively large deer populations. Populations that were destructive to winter yards causing large numbers of 6- and 8-month old fawns to die of starvation and large numbers of fawns still-born or born weak of malnourished does who scarcely survived winters themselves. But their questions and warnings went unheeded mainly because hunters were relatively happy. There were still enough quality- and trophy-class bucks to go around so Michigan remained for several more decades a leader in quality deer hunting and its DNR considered a leader in deer management.

About this same time, the department's policy on deer hunting was expanded by permitting bear hunters and then bow hunters to bait, a practice that spread like wildfire to rifle deer hunters. Other states—like Minnesota—recognized early on the problems that baiting and blinds could cause and passed preventive legislation. Not realizing the problems or choosing to ignore them, Michigan got sucked in deeper and deeper and the department began to relinquish its focus on quality deer management.

At the same time deer policy was changing, the department was growing rapidly. New, young people were hired to fill positions in the growing environmental division and vacancies left by the older fish-and-hunt crowd; most were schooled to look at environmental issues from a strict protectionist's or ecologist's point of view; many never shot a gun in their lives much less a deer.

Such changes in staff might explain the department's flip-flop on baiting. The DNR has always been against artificial feeding. They believe artificial feeding has the potential to increase deer populations beyond the carrying capacity of their range, cause disease, increase deer-vehicle accidents near feeding sites and make deer less wild and more dependent on the public. For a time the department fought the public on the issue. I remember, distinctly, a well-publicized stand the late legislator Dominic Jacobetti—a staunch believer in not shooting does and fawns—took against the department years ago by leading a group of snowmobilers to winter-feed deer in the Munising area. Eventually, the department was able to justify the practice of fall baiting by considering it a totally separate issue from winter feeding.

Today, Michigan has a large deer population, about 1.5 million that remains relatively stable except for periods when severe winters—like 1996 and 1997 which reduced the herd by about one-half million—cause fluctuations in their numbers. It also has a large number of rifle hunters, about 900,000, who hunt as permitted with bow, cross-bow, pistol, musket and rifle from October through December.

Over the years, a small but extremely important new concept— equal access to the resource—slowly filtered into DNR management policy to meet the increased demands by hunters and changes in social mores. While providing a maximum number of deer for a maximum number of hunters remained their primary goal—along with hunter safety and maintaining quality habitat—equal access to the resource became more and more important as a guiding philosophical thesis.

If a department goal was safety, then bait-blind hunting is safer. Unless one trips over a pumpkin in the bait pile or runs the ATV into a tree, the odds of getting hurt are slim to none. Aside from gun handling, safety was never a prerequisite in hunting. Since its inception, courage, stamina, intrepidity, grit and guts were considered second nature to the hunt—essential character builders. Danger and a high degree of risk were always part of the challenge.

Like the department's approval of baiting, its adoption of equal access seemed harmless and a noble goal. Who would defy equal access to a public resource? But, unlimited baiting, equal and easy access to comfortable blinds and the DNR's maintenance of a young-buck harvest proved a fatal combination for conventional hunting. Who would believe a deer management strategy that simplifies the process of hunting by producing a product that—although of poorer quality—is safer to achieve, easier to achieve and more accessible to those involved would be so destructive?

The concepts sounded good.

Certainly more equal and accessible.

About this same time—30 years ago—public educators adopted a similar philosophy with similar objectives which, on analysis, affords some interesting insight into what occurred in game management when they shifted to a philosophy of easy access and equality to all. In many public schools, discipline policies, attendance policies and tardy policies were "carefully" examined in light of progressive education theories and their once-rigid standards lowered to meet real or perceived needs of the children. Academic standard were lowered to meet these real or perceived needs as well.

As standards dropped so did expectation and effort. In the short span of 20 years or less, the goals of making learning easier and more accessible were achieved. When all was said and done, there was a dramatic rise in school crime, drug use, teen pregnancies, teen abortions, discipline problems, drop-out problems and tardy problems. The accompanying nose-dive in academic achievement was anti-climatic and often lost in the swirling, every-day pedagogic quagmire. *But, "education" was more accessible and easier to achieve.* This sad era in public education is described by many as the "Dumbing Down of America."

DNR administrators probably believed they reached the heights of compassion in substituting equality and quantity for quality and ethical hunting standards. Nothing is more sanctioned today, it seems, than public policy expressing equality except perhaps one that mitigates ethical standards. A common response when pressed to support this gentler, egalitarian shooting sport is, "It's not a shooting sport; it's hunting. Really, who's to say what a quality hunting experience is? Plus, it liberates hunters from the ethical constraints of the past, many of which are not possible to achieve today." I think the following passage from Ortega's, *Meditation on Hunting* is a proper response to such inane platitudes:

> One should not look for perfection in the arbitrary, because in that dimension there is no standard of measure; nothing has proportion nor limit, everything becomes infinite, monstrous, and the greatest exaggeration is at once exceeded by another.

When Ortega wrote these words over 50 years ago, hunters in Spain—like all of western Europe—were beginning to feel the effects of a universal rights movement. He recognized such movements were not new but only one step in the normal pattern of cultural evolution that occurred in all rich, historical cultures at some point before they started to decay as civilizations.

The movement started earlier in western Europe and continues unabated today. As I write, my radio reports the English parliament passed legislation calling for the confiscation and registration of all guns. This follows earlier attempts to have fox hunting outlawed. Is there an older, more cherished hunting tradition anywhere in the world than fox hunting in England? Could even Ortega have guessed such an action were possible?

By permitting the unregulated use of bait and blinds, the DNR redefined hunting and opened the door to one and all. Deer hunting today in Michigan is truly available to everyone with most any weapon: the kids, a spouse, a mother, father, grandpa, grandma, the infirm and handicapped. Anyone, no matter how young or old, serious hunter and not-so-serious hunter, has access to a comfortable blind to shoot or help shoot a deer. If we continue down this equality-of-hunting road we can kiss any form of traditional hunting good-bye; be content and satisfied with does, spikes and fork-horns or say hello to more and more private hunt clubs and shooting preserves.

Dumbing Down Deer Hunting

Dumbing Down Deer Hunting

PROBLEMS WITH SOCIAL SCIENCE MANAGEMENT🦌

T he DNR's adoption of a more progressive, social-science management style was probably the result of a long string of unpredictable incidents rather than planned design. In large resource agencies, such contingent events include a variety of moral, scientific and economic concerns that—through various political avenues—nudge management into new pathways with cascading consequences that produce outcomes vastly different from any predicted and often, compromised their mission.

POLICY PROBLEM # 1: SOCIAL SCIENCE MANAGEMENT IS AR-BITRARY INCONSISTENT AND DISCRIMINATORY

To help understand why a government agency would condone such a destructive practice as bait-blind hunting,

111

one must examine management changes that occur when an equal rights philosophy is adopted as a guiding management theme. The department's most serious trouble comes from the their arbitrary application of categorical rights to selective wildlife species or ecological concepts.

Equal or categorical rights grant "just" and/or "legal status" to individuals, groups, animals or any other organism, object or concept. They are usually prescribed by department fiat in response to political pressure from special interests like crop damage and block permits designed to alleviate farm-crop damage for farmers or DNR-endorsed projects like their species recovery experiments with wolves, moose, elk and other selected species.

The problem with thinking along these lines is deciding who or what is entitled to a righteous status; whether a privilege designation is more justified and thereby subject to a lesser status and less strict rules—such as rules governing the riding of bikes compared to the driving of automobiles; who in society should make these judgments and who is responsible should the programs have significant unforeseen consequences.

Categorical status for bait-blind hunting occurred by default rather than planned design; an offspring of one of those long string of unpredictable incidents that get

112

nudged into new pathways with cascading consequences. But it's important to understand that problems related to bait-blind hunting are not unique to the practice of bait-blind hunting. A brief overview of the department's predator recovery program will illustrate similar unintended consequences that reflect a systemic problem within the DNR's management style.

Some years ago, the standard defense or argument for reintroducing predators took on an ecological tone, with wolves, pine martens and fishers having "rights" to the range they once occupied. This adoption and defense of animal by way of their "rights" is the same defense the department applies to their policy of bait-blind hunting. The answer—"It's not a shooting sport; it's hunting. Who's to say what a quality hunting experience is?"— with only slight modification illicits a very similar response, "Who's to say what animals have a right to live in Michigan?"

The animals-with-ecological-rights movement had its beginning as part of a much broader environmental movement in the 1960s that flourished in the '70s and '80s with a feverish effort to instill ecological principles into many disciplines like environmental education, environmental land planning, environmental architecture, environmental this and environmental that. Everything was measured within the confines of an ecological yardstick.

During the first half of the 20th century, Roosevelt's "Wise Use" philosophy which emphasized the wise use of resources for the maximum number of people for the longest period of time—a distinctly anthropomorphic, man-centered philosophy—dominated the conservation movement. Conservation in the second half was guided by Aldo Leopold—recognized by many as the father of modern-day wildlife management—whose philosophical ethic emphasized ecology, preservation and biodiversity; a focus on nature where the land functioned as a dynamic, living system with wildlife and man intimately tied to their physical environment.

Preserving and maintaining biodiversity became important concepts because scientists recognized a natural community, rich in a variety of organisms was a healthy community and any species lost to that community had repercussions to the community, related systems and to man as well.

This ecological philosophy is generally accepted as sound science because the principles have worked for million of years throughout the evolution of human cultures and natural ecosystems. We know, for example, that within any natural community, a certain healthy dynamic equilibrium is established when diversified groups of organisms have equal opportunity for resources to enrich their lives and those of their offspring. Cultural history also suggests that equal opportunity for all within a democratic, free-market system works well for humans to enrich their lives and those of their offsprings.

So, on analysis, the questions should not be with predator protection or the reintroduction of wildlife but with their categorical rights to the land in a shrinking, man-dominated ecosystem: Which species, how many and where to introduce them? What effects their introduction might have on established game species? What possible consequences could result to established hunting traditions? And who should apply such sanctions, the Environmental Protection Agency, the DNR, the general public or whom?

Equal rights for animals and equal rights for bait-blind hunters sound good, but their very sanction by the DNR gives them precedence over all other forms of rifle hunting or, in the case of predators, the "rights" of wolves, pine martens and fishers take precedence over the "rights" of grouse, woodcock, rabbits and hares. This line of argument arbitrarily singles out one group to be promoted and leaves others to be demoted.

Any policy that makes one practice categorically more important than another risks reaching the point of huge sacrifices to traditional customs for questionable benefits the upstart might provide. Bait-blind hunting is a classic example. In setting aside centuries-old hunting ethics for less restrictive standards, the DNR caused significant harm to rifle deer hunting by:

- Eliminating the practice of fair chase from rifle deer hunting;
- Denigrating white-tailed deer as sporting animals;
- Helping to create a negative hunting image with the public;
- Elevating the practice of bait-blind hunting from vice to virtue and portraying it as a "quality hunting experience;"
- Encouraging the possible spread of disease and parasites in deer herds;
- Helping to disrupt deer travel behavior throughout the fall season;
- Helping to cause disparity in the age structure of bucks in deer herds and possibly creating problems related to an extended rut;
- Reducing quality deer-hunting habitat;
- Encouraging similar questionable hunting practices in young hunters; and
- Promoting divisive and illegal behavior among hunters.

116

While the dramatic effects of bait-blind practices on hunting are easy to document, others—related to the predator recovery program—are less dramatic but just as significant, especially the impact of wolves on the age classes of deer essential to Michigan deer hunters. David Mech, a renowned wildlife biologist with the Department of the Interior, found deer mortality from wolf predation in the central Superior National Forest in northeastern Minnesota is second only to winter weather. In his book, *The Wolf*, he states,

> Wherever wolves are controlling the numbers of their prey, they do so primarily by removing the young from the herd. . . . an estimated 62% or more of the moose killed (on Isle Royale) by wolves throughout the year were calves, and in Algonquin Park, Pimlott considered that fawns composed about 55% of the deer killed per year. It is only logical that mortality of young would have the most influence in population control by wolves because (1) this age class is almost always by far the largest in the population and thus could cause a great increase in any herd if not trimmed down, and (2) with young animals, many more individuals would have to be killed to fulfill the wolf's food requirements because of the great size difference between young and adults.

If the average wolf consumes approximately 35 deer per year and there are 150 wolves in the UP—a 1997 DNR estimate—then we can assume about 2,900 fawns will be consumed in 1998, half of which will be bucks. The old cliché: "Wolves only take the young and old" is also deceiving because it suggests "the old" are somehow useless, diseased or of little value and wolves help cultivate a healthy herd by such selective predation

In his book, Mech references a study conducted by D. H. Pimlott carried out in Algonquin Park, Ontario, which showed 46 percent of 331 adult deer killed by wolves were between the ages of 4.5- and 7.5-years of age while only 15 percent were between the ages of 1.5- and 3.5-years old. The study showed an old-animal kill rate of 66 percent if 8.5-years old and older animals were included.

On the surface, the data support the theory that wolves help the herd by preying mainly on the old, but in northern Michigan, our largest bucks fall into this 4.5- to 7.5-years old range and we don't consider them old and useless. We consider them mature and highly desirable for hunters and the social dynamics of the herd. Pimlott's studies also indicate adult bucks form a significant percentage of deer killed by wolves, roughly 55 percent. So, of the remaining 2,300 deer expected to be harvested by wolves in the UP in 1998, one can expect 1,265 to be bucks, many in the mature class range.

It might be interesting to compare these figure with estimates of bucks harvested by hunters in the Upper Peninsula in 1998. And, these figures say nothing about the number of deer killed by coyotes, bobcats and bears. Studies by game preserve managers in Europe indicate that even foxes are able to harass and eventually kill young fawns.

Permitting predators to operate unregulated may be justified in large wilderness areas where human activity is at a minimum and where hunting is strictly controlled, but it's reasonable to question such a practice where there is little wilderness left, hunter density is extremely high, hunting seasons extend for months and the predator is in direct competition with the same age classes of animals as man or with fawns soon to make up those age classes.

The same can be said with reintroducing pine marten and fishers or condoning bait-blind hunting. They may be justified but when rabbit populations and grouse populations fail to cycle in their normal fashion for 20 years and traditional rifle hunters can no longer practice their avocation, it is time to question the practice of extending rights to every animal or activity that seems like a good idea.

And if wolves have occupational-rights, why not bring back the Eastern cougar, a species as majestic and beautiful as the wolf with just as much historical right to the land? Or, why not make another effort at returning the woodland caribou, or bring in wolverines and settle the debate once and for all to whether Michigan is a wolverine state. Or, if the DNR was really interested in biodiversity why not burn a few thousand acres for our lost sharptail and prairie chicken?

Throughout the Northeast and northern Midwest were huge blocks of prairies that thrived for decades on cutover and burned-over lands. These mid-successional habitats varied in composition, depending on soil texture, topography, drainage, weather and so forth. For example, many thousand of square mile of sandy, glacial outwash plains generated the Northern Pine Barrens or Jack Pine Plains, home to lichens, mosses, hard grasses, braken ferns, sweet ferns and blueberries.

Here, scattered specimens or clusters of sugar plum, shadbush, Jack pine, cherry, aspen, and oak offered pockets of shade and cover for song birds, small mammals, deer, foxes, coyotes, sharp-tailed grouse and, in very large openings, prairie chicken. This ecosystem, like other grassy-herbaceous ecosystems, provided unique sources of biodiversity but little or no effort was made by governmental agencies to maintain their special attributes. If a DNR goal is to extol the virtues of biodiversity then they should be consistent: Why let large, wonderful tracts of biotically diverse habitats be completely lost then turn around and fight to introduce one or two species?

While the core issue here is the lack of foresight involved in the management of bait-blind hunting and predator recovery—one growing by default, the other as planned experiments—they are but two examples of the DNR's inability to precisely apply ecological principles, accurately project program outcomes or formulate effective evaluation procedures to accurately assess their progress. Many other example are available.

A similar story could be told of the department's ecological wisdom in promoting deer harvest regulations that, for over the last 60 years, generated a large deer herd, a large number of relatively satisfied hunters and huge revenues for the state. Though successful in the eyes of many, others argue the department's deer management plan was and is destructive in ways other than bait-blind hunting. They question the department's ethics in creating deer populations that lacks quality and harmony in its social structure and are far beyond the carrying capacity of their winter ranges, resulting in serious repercussions to fawn production and fawn survival during long winters.

Here, again, the DNR should be consistent. To extol the virtues of sound, scientific game management practices such as harvesting does and fawns while permitting the excessive harvest of bucks and exceptionally large herds for decades is totally incongruous. Arbitrary, categorical thinking in a world of diminishing returns is dangerous. Programs adopting such strategies should be undertaken only after very careful consideration and communication with all involved and, with some sort of binding insurance policy to trash the program if it fails or make significant corrections for its success should the program began to falter.

POLICY PROBLEM # 2: SOCIAL SCIENCE MANAGEMENT IS TOO INCLUSIVE AND MULTIPLIES PROBLEMS

Comparing the rights of bait-blind hunters and predators illustrates a major problem with social-science management: policies have a tendency to creep, become more inclusive and multiply in number, making quality game management extremely difficult to accomplish. By becoming more socially sensitive, the DNR embarked on a management style resembling the "muddling-through" tactics so destructive to public schools in their attempt at making education easy and more accessible.

Muddling-through—a process business textbooks call "disjointed incrementalism"—is really not a derogatory or disparaging phrase but rather the best I could find to describe a process that multiplies problems while attempting to solve them, a common practice when making small adjustments in a system that is inherently flawed. Muddling-through is common with equal rights initiatives because the movement has two major philosophical defects: first, the philosophy is by definition expansive, with equal rights to all and everything a movement mantra; second, the movement is based on emotion, driven by politics and generally unsupported by empirical scientific studies or historically sound, accepted practices.

Being all-inclusive and lacking sound foundations, efforts to adopt the philosophy eventually crumble or become exceptionally difficult and costly to manage because they slowly expand and grow beyond original design parameters or objectives. The last chapter pointed out numerous problems with bait-blind hunting, several of which exemplify the multiplying effect of muddling-through. Limiting the volume of bait to 10 gallons—or 8 gallons or 6.128 gallons—is a classic example of spending endless man-hours discussing a topic that would drive enforcement officers crazy and does nothing to solve the real problem which is baiting.

Not volume!

Baiting!

As mentioned, equal-oriented programs are by definition all-inclusive. Consequently, any parameters designed to meet the all-inclusive criterion must be elastic or flexible enough to accommodate groups with similar needs and agendas. We have documented how bait-blind hunters stretched the concept of rifle deer hunting to the limits of reason and beyond. Stretching the rules seems routine with all forms of deer hunting. Bow hunters, rifle hunters, musket hunters and cross-bow hunters operate, for the most part, unrestrained and often beyond the original design capacity of the weapons or the original hunting ethics contemplated for the sport. Really, what difference is there between a modern in-line musket with scope and a cartridge rifle with scope? The wonderful idea of hunting with primitive flintlock has completely lost its relevance and charm by unregulated commercialism.

Another example of hunting-style proliferation was the approval—in the spring of 1998—of elevated blinds for rifle deer hunting by Michigan's Natural Resources Commission. Strong arguments that elevated blinds would cause more accidents and were dangerous to the logging industry were ignored to give hunters one more advantage over whitetail.

It's amazing that proponents of the spear, sling shot, blow-gun and sling have not applied for admission to the club. I am sure a modern wrist rocket mounted with 4-power scope could drop a deer at bait set to 20 yards. Or, if hunters really need more advantages, why not expand rifle deer hunting to include night hunting. A special license would generate more money for the DNR and stimulate the economy with less down-time for vacations. The idea may seem outlandish but so did bait-blind hunting 20 years ago. This proliferation of deer hunting styles is on a very slippery slope, indeed.

Just as there are few regulations on bait, rifles, bows or muskets, there are no enforced regulations on blinds relative to size, contents, number of occupants and so on. Old camps, barns, farm houses and trailers work well. In fact anything and everything with a roof, including residential homes are used. A law enforcement officer's nightmare!

POLICY PROBLEM # 3: SOCIAL SCIENCE MANAGEMENT LACKS
VISION AND LEADERSHIP

Another sure sign of muddling-through—a third major flaw with many social-directed programs—is the politically correct management-by-consensus. It seems the concept of equal rights demands equal access not only to end products or resources but equal access by all to all aspects of game management.

Consensus management is used to arrive at decisions by general agreement among participants, a strategy that works well where there is *strong leadership*, clear goals or objectives and all involved are knowledgeable and experienced with the implementation process and their role in the process. But, the process is self-defeating for the DNR where deer management goals are unclear, public communication spotty, strong leadership lacking, policy implementation fragmented and recommendations by knowledgeable biologists suppressed, ignored or rejected and replaced with less credible proposals.

Michigan's deer management policy 30 years ago was a policy with an attitude. Game biologists were the professionals and, as such, dictated policy that—because of their research and expertise— was assumed good for the deer herd. I recall a wildlife biologist from Seney Wildlife

Refuge—visiting our conservation class at Northern Michigan University in the early 1960s—making a statement like, "This is how it is with deer and this is how they should be managed." Direct, to the point and authoritative. Decisions were based on sound scientific research and the biological need of game.

Today, management by consensus means a more open management style, a blend of science and sociology with changes based on scientific research, biological needs and social trends with scientific research often taking a back seat to social imperatives. Leadership consists of bringing hunters, landowners and other interested parties together to share knowledge and make decisions. Sort of a "one-big-happy-family" approach where all become sensitive to the needs and goals of others. A common directive from DNR personnel during these meetings is "It's your deer herd. What do you want us to do with it?"

There is nothing wrong with this approach to management if biologists did not lose sight of their primary goal which is game management: the job of providing quality hunting opportunities for deer, grouse, rabbits, hares, woodcock and other game species. But I believe game management and the concept of a quality hunting experience were buried as biologists became more and more involved with a host of special interest groups, all intent on imposing their will on the resource. In the struggle, ethical hunting styles and game species became subordinate to the interests of those with more political clout: neither traditional hunters nor game managers had the leadership skills or the determined focus on game and ethics to protect the sport in such a public arena.

Except to harvest large numbers of antlerless deer under controlled conditions, no committed game manager would ever recommend the use of artificial bait and blinds as methods of harvesting white-tailed deer. With the practice at the disastrous level it is in 1998, department officials either lacked the political gumption to publicly fight the trend or bought into the equality-for-all philosophy or used the management-by-consensus route to suggest the department is doing what the public wants and therefore is not culpable if rifle deer hunting is a mess.

Lack of accountability is a big problem with management-by-consensus when leadership and decision-making are abdicated to detached groups or departments. "It's not our fault, the problem originates in Lansing," is a common refrain heard by many sportsmen. Regardless, the DNR is at fault and should be held accountable for the bait-blind debacle.

Committed hunters should expect game biologists to be in the forefront of game management: leaders armed with the latest knowledge in quality game management; leaders willing to stand up for quality, ethical game management in the face of public pressure to change; proficient leaders who understand the social consequence of unethical game management and constantly press for exemplary programs.

To let them weasel out of that responsibility with inept excuses like "It's your deer herd and we are only doing what you want" is irresponsible on their part but more so on our part. If that's the kind of leadership we get for our money, we could hire a polling firm to run the department.

"We're only doing what the public wants?"

What a crock!

Where are Ralph McMullen, Pete Petoskey and John Ozoga when you need them?*

The old fish-and-hunt crowd didn't need public surveys to know what's best for deer.

---

*Ralph McMullan was a very effective director of Michigan's DNR from 1965 through 1972. Pete Petoskey was head of the department's wildlife division from 1970 through 1975 and John Ozoga conducted research on white-tailed deer at the Cusino Wildlife Research Station, Singleton, Michigan, from 1964 through 1994.

They studied deer, then conducted surveys.

More importantly, they kept their focus on game and quality hunting experiences. But, thing are different now. Rifle deer hunting and game management have been redefined. Rifle deer hunting in Michigan is primarily a bait-blind shoot and our deer policy based on social-science management with equal rights for all species of flora and fauna and equal access by all to all aspects of the planning process. In the end, hunters are left with little or no small game program and an old deer policy of cropping young animal that offers little satisfaction except to provide a large yearly crop of young animals.

POLICY PROBLEM # 4: SOCIAL SCIENCE MANAGEMENT PROMOTES PRESERVE HUNTING

In this chapter, I've tried to make the point that problems with bait-blind hunting are primarily a function of the DNR's management style which, in general is:

- Arbitrary and discriminatory in selecting and promoting programs;
- Inconsistent in applying ecological principles such as biodiversity to programs; and,
- Inconsistent in applying scientific wildlife management principles to game management.

In addition, by adopting and incorporating the equal-rights philosophy, deer management became more tortuous and circuitous with the department:

- Setting aside decades-old ethical hunting standards to allow for less restrictive regulations;
- Opening deer hunting to a host of new harvest techniques and programs, all with less strict standards;
- Permitting deer policy to creep and grow to the point where implementation became fragmented, time consuming and very difficult to carry out;
- Relinquishing their leadership and decision-making roles to marginal, non-professional interests groups with little concern for quality, ethical game management; and
- Making accountability difficult to measure.

Ortega's observation that "in the arbitrary ... there is no standard of measure; nothing has proportion nor limit, everything becomes infinite, monstrous, and the greatest exaggeration is at once exceeded by another" seems an accurate description of DNR's deer policy in the last 30 years.

Aldo Leopold stated the problem somewhat differently. Over 50 years ago—in his classic book, *A Sand County Almanac*—he recognized what can happen to hunters or professional land managers when they lower their standards and submit to the demands of recreational hunting: "The trophy-hunter is the caveman reborn. Trophy-hunting is the franchise of youth, racial or individual, and nothing to apologize for . . . in whom the capacity for isolation, perception, and husbandry is undeveloped, or perhaps lost. He is the motorized ant who swarms the continents before learning to see his own back yard, who consumes; but never creates outdoor satisfactions. For him the recreational engineer dilutes the wilderness and artificializes its trophies in the fond belief that he is rendering a public service."

With no leadership and no clear standards, rifle deer hunting was left to drift and become more and more commercialized. The rigid code that satisfied the moral concerns of those less inclined to hunt for centuries was smothered under the weight of:

More and more bait.

More and more blinds.

More and more sophisticated weapons and gadgets.

The core concept of fair chase—like the core concept of academic excellence which was lost in the "Dumbing Down of America"—was lost in the "Dumbing Down of Deer Hunting." In the process, Michigan slowly evolved into one gigantic quasi-public hunting preserve-type operation. An operation where license fees pay DNR salaries to set minimum "club" standards and hunters foot the artificial-feed bill for deer harvested during the fall shoot.

Reserve shooting, so common throughout Europe, was adopted and embraced by commercial hunting preserves in the U.S. where the term "shoot" was altered to the more appealing "hunt." Few differences exist between most preserve hunts and bait-blind hunts: animals are trained to frequent areas with planted or cast bait, then harvested by hunters from blinds or stands during the prescribed shoot.

Not long ago, sportsmen shooting preserve game were considered trophy hunters, generally described as wealthy individuals hunting trophy animals from comfortable facilities in the company of guides. Such characterization was usually justified when discussing Safari Club International hunts, but in today's economy that image could represent millions of hunters who search for trophy game all across North America.

At one time northern Michigan was a haven for large trophy whitetail but that reputation is history like the old definition of trophy hunter. Today, any animal, even a spike or fork, will do. Not only have we dumbed downed deer hunting but in the process elevated the spike and fork to a trophy-class animal. Some circumstances justify harvesting spikes, forks or antlerless deer, but, as a steady diet, year after year and for future generation?

No!

No!

The combination of bait-blind hunting, decades of harvesting young bucks, misguided and weak leadership have also promoted by default the proliferation of private hunting preserves and hunt clubs. In 1997, for example, Michigan issued 531 permits to own captive whitetails. For those in search of a reasonable trophy, the high-fence hunting industry seems the only future option where even a reasonable animal is expensive. Brochures and advertisements from commercial operations suggest a hunt for deer scoring 150 B&C (Boon and Crocket scoring) runs between $2,500 and $4,000; bucks scoring 170 B&C will cost $8,000 or more and those in the 200-class going for over $30,000. Expensive? Sure, but many hunters will find the option attractive given the alternative of paying taxes on a camp and good but non-productive hunting land.

Dumbing Down Deer Hunting

WE ALL SHARE
IN THE BLAME 🦌

T he phrase "Dumbing Down America" has a broader meaning than public education producing a generation of functional illiterates. The phrase also implies that a large percentage of the popular media, schools of higher education as well as many moms and pops are willing accomplices in the process.

Michigan deer hunters also are active participants in "Dumbing Down Deer Hunting." Even though DNR personnel are the experts and should provide strong leadership, not all the blame goes to them. We, the hunting establishment, must accept our fair share.

An interesting feature in the public's response to both the educational problem and the bait-blind issue is that of denial, denial that the problems exist. For example, the public's response to all the empirical evidence showing drastic declines in academic standards has been to ignore them or dispassionately agree but make an exception for their school.

The same contradiction and denial exist with bait-blind hunting. University wildlife management personnel, while not eager to promote bait-blind hunting, are willing to justify the practice as politically correct and ethical in that it subscribes to the concept of equal, universal rights. It fits their philosophical agenda. This also seems to be the attitude of other pro-hunting organizations in Michigan, including the Michigan Sportsmen Congress, Quality Deer Management Associations and the Michigan United Conservation Clubs.

A theory in the social sciences —"cognitive dissonance"—may offer some insight into the problem and some possible avenues of resolution. The theory suggests people are motivated not so much in being right but in believing they are right or wise or decent or good. Studies in cognitive dissonance show the deeper a belief is imbedded in one's psyche, the greater the tendency to reject and deny rational evidence to the contrary. To one degree or another, we try to justify our questionable behavior or promote our good behavior. Being "stubborn," "headstrong," "obstinate" or "contumacious" are terms used to describe this common trait. Humans as a rule are not rational but tend to rationalize. It's the kind of conundrum we see in the bait-blind hunting debate.

"What the heck, everyone else is doing it."

"The extra bait helps during the winter."

"It's a great, safe place to start the kid hunting."

Typical comments and, for the most part, behavior that helps maintain self-esteem—but such behavior can be self-defeating when the process of promoting and protecting cherished views prevents one from learning important facts or from finding real solutions to problems. The problems surrounding bait-blind hunting are too serious to permit apathy or fear of reprisal to govern and limit our response.

Many retired wildlife biologists, some active biologist and many older hunters seem confused and perplexed with bait-blind hunting. They express concerns that borders on fear for the future of rifle deer hunting. Many quit rifle deer hunting or switched to bow hunting. A few who carry enough emotional baggage on how "hunting use to be" find it difficult to even discuss the subject. Traditional hunters (like traditional public school teachers and many university professor who tried to maintain academic standards) are caught in a bind. Those who try bucking the trend find it impossible. Without leadership from the top it is just a lot easier to "join the club." Many traditional hunters have joined the bait-blind hunt club rather than fight the trend.

The hunting media must bear some responsibility as well. On Sunday, February 22, 1998, on its Outdoors page, *The Mining Journal* in Marquette carried the following quote by its outdoor writer relative to the elevated blind debate: "A few weeks ago I questioned the value of conducting such a meeting in Marquette. I hope readers didn't interpret that questioning as a statement against elevated blinds, because it really doesn't matter to me. If hunters want to climb a tree with a gun or build a UP Taj Mahal in a mighty oak to shoot at deer from, so what." Whether this accurately reflects the attitude of Michigan's outdoor journalists toward blinds is difficult to say since few offer such forthright opinions in print.

While the DNR's endorsement of bait-blind hunting is depressing, it's understandable given the bureaucracy involved and the imput of university thought into the system. Even the actions of hunters are understandable given the natural motivation for people to take the path of convenience, to be enticed by new gimmicks and new gadgets that make hunting easier and be lured into the use of bait and blind by the success of these practices. Their attitude is especially reasonable since all the negative social and psychological signposts related to the activity are down.

The media's silence is more difficult to understand. As skillful and knowledgeable communicators, they have a responsibility and legitimate warrant to question the morality of bait-blind hunting and provide some degree of leadership to their readers. Sports journalists and magazine editors along with outdoor writers either don't care, are unable to see the inherent problems with bait-blind hunting or refuse to address the issue for fear of causing dissension in hunting ranks. It's hard to appreciate their reticence because most must realize the serious threat to all hunters.

It is nearly impossible to find a popular hunting magazine that covers the subject in any fashion—for good or for bad—much less in detail. Even the more explicit hunting videos shy away. Perhaps the media, knowing how public opinion is influenced, decided no press is good press. What makes the academic prejudice, hunter confusion and media acquiescence or apathy for bait-blind hunting so dangerous is that they add leverage to a similar bias and apathy in Michigan's DNR .

Dumbing Down Deer Hunting

GETTING GOOD HELP

Knowing where and what the spoor
Marks the hunter's skill and score.
So said Canton, Audubon and
More.
But who will set the mark-
Extol
Atone
For men of bait and blind?
None I know.
They must write that tome
Alone.

JL

Dumbing Down Deer Hunting

THE BIG PICTURE 🦌

G iven the preceding list of grievances with bait-
blind hunting and Michigan's DNR, logic might
dictate the question: Should an attempt be made to reform
rifle deer hunting in Michigan? With bait-blind hunting's
near universal acceptance among Michigan's hunting fraternity; hunters' never-ending demand for new and
"better" hunting products; and the pervasive and appealing trend in America to dumb-down all form of traditional
values, there seems little hope for reformation.

The future is especially grim for those who cherish
the traditions and styles of classical hunting. If reform is
not possible or desirable, the problem for bait-blind hunters will be to maintain some degree of personal and collective pride within their ranks and some degree of moral
status with the non-hunting public for, in the long-run,

they will be measured as hunters more than stewards of wildlife and their habitats.

Being good stewards of the land implies a certain sensitivity and responsibility toward the resource base. We look to farmers to be good stewards of soil and water. We look to timber companies, state and federal forests management agencies to be good stewards of the forests. And, to the same degree, we look to hunters and game managers to be good stewards of game.

Since Teddy Roosevelt's day, the cooperation and cost-sharing between wildlife agencies and hunters has been outstanding. No other segment of society has done more to preserve, maintain, rebuild and purchase wildlife habitat. For decades this coalition was guided by a very simple but clear formula: quality habitat = quality game = quality hunting; the core formula of good wildlife stewardship.

But good stewardship is more than preserving, maintaining, rebuilding and purchasing quality habitat or, for most of us, contributing to the National Rifle Association or attending a Ducks Unlimited banquet. Being sensitive and responsible stewards implies moral standards be met and adhered to in every step of the stewardship transaction—a consideration especially relevant in today's society.

When game managers and hunters explain that bait-blind hunting is an effective game management tool, they never bother to explain whether we *should* hunt this way. Our focus today should not be on equal access or preservation, restoration or quality habitat but on *how we kill*—our harvest techniques define our public image; it's here the line is drawn beyond which the public sufferance for hunters erodes. It's the thin line Roosevelt, Ortega and Leopold all recognized that separates the true sportsman from meat hunter, hunting from non-hunting.

How Michigan hunters will justify to themselves and others that hunting from comfortable blinds over bait is quality hunting or part of the wildlife-stewardship formula will be interesting to note. Should they find success and comfort in such sport then they must make a clean break with the past, develop a new set of ethics and find new heroes to admire—Roosevelt, Ortega, Leopold and the catalogue of other great hunters can never serve their purpose again. They must set to work on building credibility with the non-hunting public—alone.

And they must rename their fall shooting sport; the name "deer hunting" meets none of the traditional hunting definitions and its continued use can only deceive and mislead. For hunting to be condoned it must be based on solid game management principles with a genuine respect for nature, a sincere veneration for game and the taking of game along with a clear expression of these articles of faith to the non-hunting public. The majority of non-hunters is generally tolerant but often troubled with contrived statements designed to mislead them toward our real moral intention. Calling the practice of shooting deer from blinds over bait "deer hunting" is a ruse the public will not buy.

The big push within sportsmen's organizations toward building credibility today is on educating the public about hunting's benefits and virtues. But this effort will have little effect if the core issue of the ethical taking of game is not addressed. Jim Posewitz in his wonderful little book, *Beyond Fair Chase*," gives us a modern-day definition of the ethical hunter, "A person who knows and respects the animal hunted, follows the law, and behaves in a way that will satisfy what society expects of him or her as a hunter." Given this emphasis on social expectations today, their educational focus would be better served if the spotlight were redirected back on themselves. Perhaps, before formulating their next educational package, the following survey should be sent to their members and the results judged against the line crossed between sportsmen and meat hunter.

Fellow Hunters
Please answer the following questions with the spirits of Aldo Leopold and Teddy Roosevelt looking over your shoulder.

Y   N

___ ___ Is it morally right to use piles of bait to attract and train deer to a site, then shoot them?

___ ___ Is it morally right to hide in comfortable, heated blinds and thereby deny deer their survival skills during a hunt?

___ ___ Is it morally right to use a hunting technique that disrupts deer travel patterns for several months?

___ ___ Is it morally right to use a hunting technique that helps cause great disparity in a population's sex ratio?

___ ___ Is it morally right to use a hunting technique that helps cause great disparity in a population's age ratio between bucks?

___ ___ Is it morally right to use a hunting technique that has the potential to cause disease and increase parasites in deer?

___ ___ Is it morally right to use a hunting technique that totally eliminates the concept of fair chase from hunting?

___ ___ Is it morally right to use a hunting technique that depreciates the essence and vitality of white-tailed deer?

To deny the reality of ethics in hunting is to open our-selves up to social criticism—at a time when the percent-age of hunters is on the decline—especially from the more radical anti-hunters who look for weaklinks in the sys-tem. The irony in this picture is that we invite their intru-sion by our insistence on equal access to the resource. After all, if hunters with rifles, pistols, flintlocks, bows, cross-bows, piles of bait and thousands of blinds have "rights" to shoot deer and wolves, coyotes, bobcats and bears have "rights" to kill deer, then deer must have some "right" as well. As spokespersons for deer-rights, their emotional moralizing must be considered a legitimate philosophical view on game management; and our "sound" game management techniques—like culling, har-vesting, carrying capacity—measured against their "sound" moral concepts—like the ethics of killing for sport or the morality of inflicting pain on sensitive beings.

How well the pro-hunting fraternity is able to combat the entrenched and hard-core antis—should a conflict oc-cur—is difficult to say for their emotional appeal is strong and hard to deflect. In addition, their leaders are unified and articulate, their followers well organized and backed by a sympathetic popular media and many state and federal legislators. Plus, their ability to articulate their position with emotion, their verbal dexterity in defining and redefining traditional values and their repetitious recitation of emotional messages in a unified chorus make them exceptionally formidable adversaries. This impressive list of public relations characteristics is exactly what the pro-hunting crowd, in general, and the traditional hunting crowd, in particular, sadly lack.

Fortunately, hard core anti-hunters are only a very small group, the vanguard of a movement that—at this point in time in America—could go either way on the question of hunting. Most of the non-hunting public occupy the moral middle-ground and are not zealots but rational individuals whose sense of right and wrong is governed by logic and reason. Many are friends and relatives. Most realize hunting's biological benefit but their tolerance of hunting revolves around their attitude toward hunting behavior with an emphasis on fair chase.

Their sense of right and wrong and ability to reason logically is shown in their response to the educational problem. Across the country today there's a movement, loosely referred to as "Excellence in Education," which incorporates a number of innovations like "Magnet Schools," "Charter Schools," and "Schools of Choice" that demonstrate a huge national investment of time and money to change the culture of education: efforts designed to put standards and accountability back into the educational process, a process so vital to the survival of this country.

Education was at a crossroads where it could continue down the "Path of Convenience" to the left or "Path of Credibility" to the right. Fortunately, enough Americans recognized that with standards, structure and leadership you can have both equality and quality—it just takes a lot more work and discipline on the part of all involved.

Rifle deer hunting is at the same crossroads with the same posted signs: "Path of Convenience" to the left or "Path of Credibility" to the right. Like education, its survival will depend upon how many hunters elect the path of discipline and moral responsibility or how many elect the path of convenience and expediency.

Should the "Path of Convenience" be selected, we will continue to drift toward more preserve-type hunting and risk having the non-hunting public judge us as less than honorable hunters. We must remember, non-hunters make up about 85 percent of the population and are the majority who vote on all ballot initiatives.

Should the "Path of Credibility" be chosen, hunters will need to substitute their strict "scientific" arguments for hunting with declarations that exemplify morally responsible behavior. *These declarations should be based on a new kind of ethics: standards that set limits on what we harvest to maintain the viability of deer herds—while offering adequate "trophy" potential—and clear sociological standards on how we harvest these animals.*

Then, perhaps, enough hunters will accept the challenge and petition the DNR to use its extensive species-recovery experience and institute a "Hunter Recovery Program" based on the principles of fair chase, respect for the biology and sociobiology of game, respect for land owners and fellow hunters. Surely there must be room in this large state for the still hunt, the drive and stand hunt—hunting styles that stood the test of time because they were judged by societies as honorable and morally legitimate.

There is absolutely no reason to believe Michigan hunters will not support anti-bait, anti-blind legislation for a sound quality game management plan. The spirit of resistance to unethical hunting hasn't died. It's there in all hunters to the degree they feel game deserve a fair chance. And, given the hunting fraternity is divided and marching in different directions, it's possible that a spirited group with public support can be the vanguard to quality deer management. Management that supports 1) A quality herd with a balanced social structure that includes an appropriate doe to buck ratio, fawn to doe ratio and young to mature buck ratio; 2) A quality herd that's balanced with its natural carrying capacity including adequate winter range; 3) A quality herd that's balanced with its cultural carrying capacity including adequate harvest techniques that respect hunting, logging, farming and insurance concerns; 4) Ethical and moral harvest techniques that includes fair chase and respect for the dignity of white-tailed deer, fellow hunters and land owners. In short, lets put the emphasis back on the magnificent whitetail and away from recreational hunting. Michigan sportsmen have a long history of accepting and complying with reasonable proposals. Plus, down deep, they know that eliminating bait-blind hunting is the right thing to do.

If we don't do it, who will?

If we don't do it now, then when?

A **Gourmet's** Guide to

VENISON
SAUSAGE
and

COOKING VENISON

130
Smart and
 Elegant Recipes
Simplified H ome
Sausage
 Making Technique
45 Tested Sausage
Recipes Including Hard Salami
Pepperoni - Summer Sausage - Chorizo - and Many More

$12.95

Forest Wildlife
And Ecology

A beautifully illustrated sportsmans' guide to the principles of ecology and wildlife management adaptable to school, camp or cottage.

Used In Over 150 Schools
Focus on Deer and Other Game Animals
Emphasis on Hunting and the Hunting Ethic
Teacher/Student Lab Manual Available
School Discounts

Text $13.95
Lab Manual $9.95

ORDER FORM

Woodcock Press

Shipping Address

Name _____

Address _____

City _____ State ____ Zip ____

Phone _____

A Gourmet's Guide to Venison Sausage and Cooking Venison
$12.95

==================

Forest Wildlife And Ecology
$13.95

Dumbing Down Deer Hunting
$12.95

Title	Quantity	Unit Price	Total Price

Subtotal............

Shipping and Handling ($2.50 for the
first book. 50¢ each additional book......

Total Order Amount...............

Mail this form with check or money order to Woodcock Press
13903 Summer Meadow, Rock MI 49880